Be

Be:

An Alphabet
of
Astonishment

~

Michael Lipson, PhD

for Holly, Asher and Rody

B *is for Be*

We really are here, and that is just outrageous.

I invite you to share an astonishment: that the world exists, and you in it. Not that the world is beautiful, or that you are happy, because so often it's not like that. Apart from personal troubles, we are all perpetrators and victims of global climate change, a series of endless, unprecedented crises, and an era of upheavals and painful decisions to come.

Still, you are here. The world does exist. Shakespeare still just-audibly whispers: *Thy life is a miracle.*

Even if we often mis-see this world, mis-understand it, blindly stumble past its glories and foolishly contribute to its horrors. The world may not be solid, but it is real and true. Something is here, with someone to misunderstand it, or who may come to understand it better and wake up within it. You, for instance.

Instead of getting habituated to this state of affairs, I ask you deliberately to become ever more energized by it. The direct hit of being, as a felt experience, will help you to grow increasingly free, increasingly creative, and more and more in love with this place and its inhabitants. Whoever and whatever we ultimately are.

There is a difference between one hour and another, as Ralph Waldo Emerson tells us. A difference in their authority.

Most of the time we rush around trying to get things done. We pursue the things we like and avoid the things we don't like. We waste time, too. Yet the total extent, the ultimate context within which this daily grind grinds on, and within which we ply our various trades and ride our prejudices around, strutting across the stage for a span - the context or question of its all being here in the first place - rarely stops us from the onward rush, the to-do list, what Buddhists call the world of 10,000 things.

Sometimes, through effort or through grace, through disaster or delight, or for no reason at all, the sheer factfulness of things leaps up in mastery and authority and rearranges it all with a feeling of strange evidence: *Here we are. This is happening.*

A deer outside my window stands in the garden, twitching her ears as she cheerfully destroys the buds of our carefully tended tulips. A rock drips with rainwater and glistens. The moss shines. There's an overhanging oak and the slight sway of a hemlock branch. I hear a turkey gobble in the neighbor's field. The astonishment at this scene, the weirdness that there is such a world, where all this not only could but does take place, etches and enhances every feature of the event. It morphs from everydayness into untellable significance.

Emerson again:

> *Crossing a bare common, in snow puddles, at twilight, under a clouded sky, without having in my thoughts any occurrence of special good fortune, I have enjoyed a perfect exhilaration. I am glad to the brink of fear.*

For some, amazement at existence quickly diverts into related issues and questions. "Why does the world exist?" Or, "How did it come about?" Or, "What is my own purpose on earth?" Or, "How can we preserve the earth?"

These questions can be urgent. They tend to get better provisional answers, I have found, to the degree that there's first a reverberating $\mathrm{GONG!!}$ at the point of original astonishment. Look around you. Whether it's a bustling street scene, a cozy apartment, the burden of work, or a day at the beach. What do you yourself mean by a thought like, "This stuff is here"?

In this B-first alphabet, I am suggesting that you intensify your own sense of the thereness and the hereness of things. It's not about information. You have enough information. It's about an experience.

And while I would love to tell you exactly how to go about getting such an experience for yourself, I don't think I can. I'll offer tips and occasional exercises that I hope will help, but they may all be wrong for (specifically) you. To realize the reality of this world, you'll have to marvel your own way into it.

Why is there something, when there could so easily be nothing?

The power of that famous philosophical question doesn't really lie in the "why"-part. It's in the "there is something"-part. The question makes us stand fruitfully stupefied before the uni-verse, "like the ox in front of the new barnyard gate," as farmers say. It's not just that there is something. It's that there *is* something.

I admit that I normally live in moments of weak authority, like the adolescent who crosses their arms and pouts, "I didn't ask to be born." It's what Dante called the Grand Refusal. This stance has its satisfactions: a kind of self-righteousness, the high status of victimhood, and an excuse to avoid the difficulties of engaging with the world. If I don't play, I can't lose. It's related to thoughts like these: "I know well enough that the world is and what it is. It has no more basic surprises for me. It's a mess I didn't make and shouldn't have to clean up. It's a jungle where everyone has to fight for what they want. The planet would have been better without human beings at all, and it will be better once we've finally annihilated ourselves."

We can move in the opposite direction from this stance, and allow ourselves to be shocked by the universe and grateful for it. You don't need religion to make this turn. Some of those who exist most happily and intensely are atheists, perhaps because they have the courage to face life without imaginary supports. Still, a focus on being, and even to find being as the supreme being, lies at the root of the major religious traditions.

Five hundred years ago, Leibniz came up with the "principle of sufficient reason." There must be sufficient reason for anything to come about, so there must be sufficient reason for the universe, the totality, to come about. That was his idea of the originating will that he identified with god. There does seem to be an urge or will for the universe to exist, because, well, here it all is. It wouldn't be a human will, though, or even much like a human will. No human would write the world the way it's written.

In the Jewish, Christian and Islamic traditions, for instance, the very name of god is BE. Did you think it was something else, like "God" or "Lord" or "Jesus" or "Adonai" or "Elohim" or "Allah"? By all means skip ahead to *N is for Name* to get the details, but god is actually called "Be" about 7,000 times in the Mosaic Bible, the sourcebook of all three traditions. And then there's the time Moses asks for the divine name point blank and gets "I AM" as the answer.

The shock of being is an experience. It changes everything. When the door swings open on that view, resentment vanishes, at least for moments. You find not only that the world has some life in it, but that the world is alive and meaningful through and through. You act, then, from out of the primal, primordial urge for there to be a universe at all.

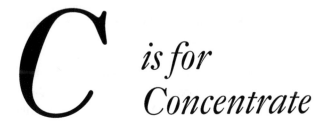

is for
Concentrate

When I rode the subway every day to work in New York City, all the way from Carroll Gardens in Brooklyn to 137th Street in Harlem, changing endlessly at the 14th Street stop from the F train to the A train, I used to read. Novels. Spirit books. Psychology.

Not exactly a library atmosphere, the A train. Often there was no place to sit; there were strangers jostling you all the time; there was stopping and starting, doors opening and closing, incomprehensible PA announcements. Sometimes panhandlers. One guy used to come into the subway car through the interconnecting doors carrying a battered saxophone. He'd put it to his mouth and start screeching on it, just a horrible sound. After a few excruciating minutes he'd pause and say, "I'll keep playing in this car this same way until somebody gives me money!" We'd all laugh and pay a little something, and off he'd go to disturb the peace in the next car. At times, though I loved the scene, I would dive deep into whatever book I had with me. I'd notice my neighbors for a while, but then drop my eyes to the page. At odd moments, I'd forget I was on the subway. I'd even forget I was turning the pages. The story in the book became foreground and the rest of life a vanishing background. Once or twice, lurching with the train's motion but not noticing it, I actually missed the subway stop for work. Then, when I realized, cursing and jumping up, it took a frustrating hour to get off at the next stop, switch to a downtown train, get off again, switch uptown, and finally get to work late, only to face my supervisor's glare.

There is one magic key to spiritual development, and it will help us in our project of intensification of being. It's the ability we all have to concentrate our minds. To be so immersed in the chapter of life we're currently reading that we forget everything else. We can take our scattered light and gather it into a laser focus. Then it has different powers. We burn a hole right through to reality.

Concentration makes concentric circles. First your mind centers around what you choose as a focus, and along with that, as part of the same gesture, your body may curve toward it. Think of a group gathered around a fire, turning their heads and bodies toward the storyteller, even unconsciously inclining one ear toward the flow of narrative.

Your heart has a way of coming along too, so that you start to love whatever things or persons or conceptual areas glow in that center – as a teacher may come to love best their one most problematic student, who has caused the most grief and taken the most time, as ants become personal to the entomologist and strips of iron to the smith. "She's coming along now," says the plumber of the water, or the shipwright of the boat.

As more and more of you participates in the act of concentration, the sense of effort dissolves. You bend to the task, while the thing you focus on grows evident, held in clarity, as you yourself are held.

With increasing devotion to anything - a scheduling problem, a piece of gravel - the circle of light also expands. It is as if an attentive world accompanies your focus. As if heaven and earth pay attention with you, and participate in the concentricity. Tennyson, talking to a flower:

> [I]f I could understand
> What you are, root and all, and all in all,
> I would know what God and man is."

An old friend, Fred Dennehy, a lawyer and litigator, once said that the famous oath to "tell the truth, the whole truth, and nothing but the truth," was unnecessary. He noticed that if a witness tells nothing but the truth, the whole truth of the case has a way of revealing itself. A pure focus resonates out to a wide circle, like the Christmas crèche that starts at the baby, then extends to include the family, the animals, the wise folk and shepherds, the angels, the starry sky.

And real concentration is improvisation. When I'm weakly concentrated on something, I find myself thinking the same thing over and over. When I am really in the topic, then memories and associations disappear. The thing becomes new. Maybe it was hard to focus at the start; now it's easy. I am surprised to find new features in a meditation theme, a face, a breath. The old boot in the mudroom, caked with mud, becomes eloquent.

What exactly are we concentrating? What is it we bring to bear on the matter at hand? We can call it mind, or attention, or we can use the traditional term, and say that we are concentrating our light.

Light is invisible. The light in outer-space, for instance. We don't see the light as it travels from the sun to the moon. We only see the lit moon, reflecting.

Physicist Arthur Zajonc of Amherst College constructed a light beam of great intensity, a laser, inside a box that had been lined with absorbent black material and made free of dust. A glass window had been set in one of the box's walls so that you could peer into it. And so, though the laser was beaming, there was nothing whatever to be seen in the box.

The light of our mind or attention is the same way. It is most noticeable when weak or troubled, flecked with the dust of our habits and worries. It is most invisible when strong. During a strong, concentrated moment of paying attention to anything, only the object of attention, the object of the light, appears. At such moments, we don't notice ourselves. Attention is selfless in this sense, and un-self-regarding.

Yet when attention becomes even stronger, something special can happen. Concentrated attention can stay un-self-regarding even as it awakens to the reality of itself and the surrounding world. That is how concentrated we want to get. That degree of concentration yields the experience of being.

C can also stand for Can.

A bunch of us at a conference were sitting around one day during a break. We found ourselves talking about why god created the world. It was that kind of conference, with the standard good-hearted but actually fruitless speculation on ultimate themes. To be fair, people did have profound and beautiful things to say about physical evolution and the evolution of the soul, about freedom, about Earth becoming the Star of Love. All of our guesses sounded a bit hollow, though, a bit tired, a bit rehearsed. As our suppositions started to sputter and die down, an awkward silence loomed. Just then Claire, who hadn't yet spoken, made a slight flourish with her hand and said, "I think he wanted to show what he can do." And we all burst out laughing. Delight in doing. And showing. We'd forgotten about that. When Claire said it, it became true. Play seemed like the obvious origin of all.

Simone Weil, the philosopher, who died in 1943, was a piercingly aware student of being. She wrote to topple Descartes' famous sentence, "I think, therefore I am," which seems to ground the self's very existence in the ability to think. She reached deeper and transformed his slogan into, "I can, therefore I am."

This is a declaration of empowerment, democratic, the discovery that we each can master that archaic flare or flair, the light gesture that started it all.

I often face patients whose fundamental sense of themselves is that they cannot. They are unable. Can't go for the desired career. Can't declare their love. Can't leave the problematic relationship. Can't confront that friend. Can't rise to the challenge of their lives.

One feature of this sense of disability is that it is also a sense of non-being. Some people hardly exist, or anyway have the feeling of disappearing, floating. They may have been catapulted into hazy, dissociated realms by early sexual or physical abuse. The world passes by like a dream or nightmare, unreal. Learned helplessness is learned disappearance.

Derealization/Depersonalization Disorder has its dual name because sufferers feel at once that they themselves do not exist and that the world around them is fading or illusory: Self and world get fake together. If things take a healthy turn, and the sufferer begins to exist, the world around them sharpens into vibrancy too.

Of all our abilities, of all the things we can, the one primal ability is precisely…that we can concentrate. What we do with our own minds is under our (partial) control, swayable by our conscious choice. Then we find: Whatever we turn toward, turns toward us. The things of the world are grateful for our attention.

Weil tells the story of a renowned 19th century priest, the Curé d'Ars. He was an uneducated farm boy with a vocation for the priesthood. In those days, you had to pass a Latin test to be a priest. He studied, but couldn't get there. He tried again. Failure. Again. Same result. He just couldn't learn Latin. Finally the local authorities realized he was a born priest and they made an exception, granting him priesthood without a successful test. Their leniency paid off. He became a beloved preacher and healer, and people came from all over France to his tiny country church.

Toward the end of his life, someone asked the Curé how he had developed his amazing psychic ability to read within the souls of those who came to him for help. Was it his fervent life of prayer that had earned him this kind of perceptive power? Oh no, he answered, it was those useless years of trying to learn Latin. As Weil tells it, "Every effort adds a little gold to this treasure, which nothing on earth can take away. The useless efforts to learn Latin made by the Curé d'Ars for long and painful years, bore all their fruit in the marvelous discernment by which he perceived the very soul of his penitents, behind their words and even behind their silences."

You can concentrate your mind. You can concentrate all the way to becoming identical with whatever you perceive or think.

That's the magic wand that turns a black-and-white world into a multiverse of living color. The wand is in your hand right now. Tap on any element of the world and it will start to shine, to speak, to be.

D *is for Desire*

I think our ache for the sense of reality is so huge that we live either in the hope of it, or in the light of it, or in the despair of it at every instant.

If our greatest, deepest, most all-pervasive desire is to exist and to know it, to feel the Earth and cosmos as real and meaningful, and to foster reality in its wholeness, coherence, vitality and signficance – why wouldn't everyone be talking about this?

Well, for one thing the quality of being is so hard to put into words or concepts that we can't quite think about it. Being, in itself, as the precondition for any content in consciousness, doesn't actually have any content – hence, no information, nothing to report.

Simone Weil again in her private Notebooks:

> *There are certain joys – and they are the most precious [my*
> *emphasis] – which, when imagined, are extremely pale;*
> *whose whole value consists in their presence itself. We lack*

16

the stimulus to seek out these pale joys, even at the cost of a
slight effort – unless…. (May I no longer commit this crime
towards myself of allowing them to slip by.)

Like the dark matter of physics, our desire for being pervades
and underlies but scarcely interacts with all the qualities and
things and events and persons of our experience. It's even more
invisible than light.

The word desire comes to us from Latin de-sidera, meaning,
from the stars. The wise ones who invented language and first
thought of desire were not focused on our exclusively local likes
and dislikes, our French fries or kale, our media preferences.
Those ancient coiners of words sensed a far wider context to
what urges us along, an overcurrent, a celestial drive.

When people feel ashamed of their wants, needs, desires,
wishes, they may be failing to realize that our little desires are
actually the outer face or distorted form of a vast background
longing that travels into us all the way from our continuity with
the stars. "We call it longing," says Robert Hass, "because
desire is filled with infinite distances."

An important Buddhist lament, the second of Buddha's Four
Noble Truths, states that the cause of all our suffering is desire.
But the Awakened One was referring, not to desire in our
starry sense, but to attachment. What I'm attached to on Earth
is doomed. Time sweeps it away. Attachment is the state in
which we think we can get something and keep it. Or that
something belongs to us. When we don't merely hold and
cherish, but clutch. In our lives of getting, getting, getting, it
can be hard to see that the sport is always one of catch and
release, whether we like it or not. Time, if nothing else, will
loosen our grip.

A patient of mine was well placed to have sex with many famous and beautiful women in the 1950's. He did so, extensively and rapturously. He was gorgeous himself, too, back then. When I knew him though, the years had been wearing him down pretty unrapturously. He was in his 80's and falling apart. His only topic in therapy was his agony over those women: How great it had been, and how he wasn't getting any anymore, and how it could never happen again. Over and over, like a personal hell. Attachment = unwise.

On the other hand, attachment can be seen as the most beautiful thing, the very seal on reality. Someone who cannot grieve, who cannot ache with loss, is someone who has tried too hard to stay unwoundable. When we give our heart wholly to a person, a project, a community, a cause, then one measure of our giving may be precisely the extent to which we are heartbroken if the cause founders, if the person dies, if the community crumbles.

There's a Zen story in which a master is found weeping after his son has died. His disciples remind him that he taught them not to be attached to earthly things, which are all transient and illusory. "Yes," says the master, "but the death of my son is a super-illusion."

Imaginative literature has often dealt with this theme in its own ways, and we can hardly take them with adequate seriousness. Think of the Tin Man in *The Wizard of Oz*, who says, "Now I know I have a heart, because it's breaking." And Pinocchio, whose quest is to become a real boy. In the end, it happens precisely when he can weep with compassion and act courageously to save his own father, the wood carver.

These fictional accounts lay out a truth we all know but may never consider: The degree to which someone or something is real is itself not a fixed quantity, but a variable one.

When we totally involve ourselves in what we want, as W. H. Murray wrote, things happen to aid us. We make our own desiring presence in the universe more existent, more evident, more real. Our commitment torques the cosmos and invites a huge, often quite practical, assent. Murray was writing about the start of a Himalayan mountaineering expedition:

> *We had definitely committed ourselves and were halfway out of our ruts. We had put down our passage money — booked a sailing to Bombay. This may sound too simple, but is great in consequence. Until one is committed, there is hesitancy, the chance to draw back, always ineffectiveness. Concerning all acts of initiative (and creation), there is one elementary truth, the ignorance of which kills countless ideas and splendid plans: that the moment one definitely commits oneself, then Providence moves too. All sorts of things occur to help one that would never otherwise have occurred. A whole stream of events issues from the decision, raising in one's favour all manner of unforeseen incidents and meetings and material assistance, which no man could have dreamt would have come his way. I learned a deep respect for one of Goethe's couplets: "Whatever you can do or dream you can, begin it. Boldness has genius, power and magic in it!"*

Murray knew that the universe is ready for us. It lends an ear and a hand when we are definite about our aim. Or so it seems. But looking at it another way, the stars as organizers of destiny ("Providence" according to Murray) are themselves the desire that rises in us. It is as if our total self, our hidden constitution, extends at least to the realm of the stars — not the stars of natural science, those dead bodies of gas far away in outer space, but rather the stars as living beings within us.

Rainer Maria Rilke, in the early 20th century, was handling a human skull one day and looking at the craggy lines where the plates of bone close together. He had the weird idea that those lines could be the grooves for a potential phonograph needle - a newish invention at the time. If such a needle could play along the skull-lines and the sound were amplified, it would produce a unique melody.

What if you could relax the plate tectonics of the skull and let them continually reorganize, if only slightly, imperceptibly, in accordance with the circling of the stars? Then Rilke's melody of the skull-lines would become an endless improvisation, flowing in from the ever-changing music of the spheres.

Please put down the book after this paragraph and look around a bit, then consider (yes, also from sidera, stars). Sense your way to the boundary of the room or landscape in which you are sitting. Let it be as if your body expands like a balloon to fill the space you are in, mingling with everything there while retaining its invisible and distinct coherence. Then let this aspect of yourself expand still further and extend beyond that, down to the earth and up through the sky and out beyond the visible horizon on all sides. Picture your body as an invisible, expanding light-sphere. Imagine that you are continuous in this way with the planets and stars reaching out in all directions, out and out in a huge star-sprinkled open space on all sides. Feel yourself "embracing and embraced," as Rilke once put it. Sense your way into the aliveness of this galaxy-permeating space, and feel what there is to feel there. Declare yourself within it, as if you were to say to all of space and time, "Here I am. Take note of me." And see if that community of lights responds to you – most likely not in words, but still in some intelligible sugges-tion, maybe a nudge of "Yes."

Now gently return to your normal body limits, the familiar physical you. Give thanks that there actually is this place in which you find yourself. Let your huge reach fade away, leaving you with an enhanced but entirely local presence.

Desire. Desiderata. Consider. Sidereal. The stars are always wheeling around through the sky, unseen and seen, way above and way below our feet and on all sides, and the earth's slow wobble makes them wheel still more. The pole star, the North Star by which we guide ourselves on earth, and which the other stars seem to circle, is a relative newcomer, not a nail securely fastened to the firmament. A few thousand years ago, the Earth's pole pointed out toward Vega, in the Lyre – a completely different star. A few thousand years hence, it will point somewhere else. Attachment = unwise.

Wishes, wants and desires are especially important to me because of my son Asher, who died when he was 25 years old. He's the Zen master's "super-illusion" that makes me weep - and laugh, too. When Holly and I were finally going through his things more than a year after he died, we came upon a birthday card he had once written to Rody, his younger brother,

> *Brave Brother!*
> *may all of your days be joyous,*
> *and may you seize with ferocity*
> *all that you desire!*

Asher was our desire, and sometimes I just don't believe he's gone. Physically. I want him here physically - standing in the open door of the fridge and grazing the raspberries right out of the box. We had 25 years in which to love him, not guessing until the cancer diagnosis that he wasn't here to be seized or grasped by us. He won't sit with us and build his hilarious air castles; he won't share his eclectic musical tastes or his concern for prisoners' rights, his climate anxiety, his love of bonsai trees. I'll haul him into this alphabet from time to time because, living and dying, he taught me singular lessons about how to be.

E *is for Eyes*

The first language, the word that calls us to Earth, is spoken through the eyes, from mother to child.

We can ask, "What is it, exactly, that the new mother communicates to the new child through prolonged eye-contact?" Or, "What is it that the child communicates back?"

And I suppose we can answer by saying there is warmth there, and wonder, and relief that the birth has occurred, and often an atmosphere of love and joy that surpasses all previous experience. The mother sees the child into existence. "Here you are," her eyes more-than-say, "Welcome to earth." But such paraphrases never hit the mark. They can't convey what the shared glance conveys so lightly and fully.

One day when Asher was just three, my wife Holly was bathing him in the bathtub of our first Brooklyn apartment. As he splashed his face, she warned him, in that way we speak to kids: "Be careful with your eyes, Asher, because what are eyes for?" Asher looked up at her through lashes that had matted into starbursts from the water and said, "For loving."

Somehow, this magic of early eye contact fades with time, disappears, goes sour. Our gaze wanders off. We start to avoid each other; later we drop our heads, ashamed. Norman Mailer said that when two men pass each other on the street and their eyes meet, one of them loses. How did it descend from pure love, pure meaning, pure existence-bestowing between mother and child, and collapse down into competition, shame, and fear?

I remember as a kid I was already frightened by the eyes on some drawings that hung along the staircase in our house.

They were no ordinary drawings. They were so-called "brass-rubbings." My mother had taken rolls of tracing paper on a summer trip to England and labored for hours in church-yards to get these images. She would unroll the paper over brass carvings on certain tombs, then rub ink or charcoal over the paper, and so bring out an eerie visual echo of the carving – itself an image of the person buried in the vault beneath. Back home in the States, she hung the framed rubbings on the wall by the stairs – life-sized dead people, upright in effigy, survey-ing every trip up and down those steps. Open, staring eyes, hands in prayer on their chests. They scared me so much that Mom at one point cut out colored construction paper circles and fixed them with Elmer's glue where the pupils should have been so that the eyes would seem to stare out at me a tad less ghoulishly. It didn't work. I remember my six-year old thoughts: "Yes, but behind the dots the empty eyes are still there, staring!"

E is for Emerson, as in Ralph Waldo. He wondered about "this old uneasiness of ours," our total disappointment with life, and saw it as the negative image of "the soul's enormous claim." We sense our high standard when we experience how far the world has fallen. The fear of eyes is like that: a negative testimony to their power, which continues long after the mother-child dyad is history, and can even grow more intense through life. That's why the Sufis and even Western psychologists and the New York Times have confirmed that you can fall in love with anyone just by allowing for the right kind of eye contact. It is not the normal adult eye contact, but a much more steady, prolonged and open-minded practice.

An extreme form of this, and a kind of test case of what is at stake in eye contact, comes up in Rilke's poem, "Archaic Torso of Apollo." Time long ago lopped off the head of the statue he describes there, along with the arms and legs. All that is left is a torso. But Rilke says that it seems to him as if the gaze from those unknown eyes has gotten screwed down, like the wick in a kerosene lamp, and now it gleams out from the torso at every point. "There's not a spot here that doesn't see you," he writes, and then, abruptly: "You must change your life." The gaze does not actually require eyes, but only grows in intesnsity without them, and the eye-less seeing that radiates out from the torso works as a challenge.

What if we could allow not just the eyes of other humans or animals, or the seeing-seeming presence of the long lost eyes of some Greek statue – what if we could allow absolutely every-thing to exchange glances with us? Then the floor would be looking at you, and the sky, and the day as a whole. Then you would share the quality, the intensity, the emergent event of meeting, with everything. As Thomas Berry said: "The universe consists in a communion of subjects, not a collection of objects."

In a way, this is the world of Curious George. Carried aloft by helium balloons, he eventually alights on a street lamp and causes quite a stir in the street scene below. The humans and horses notice him, but so do the automobiles that also look up toward him with their headlights, surprised and tickled by the floating monkey. Everything is alive. Everything has its glance and its opinion.

Freud said religious sentiment was like paranoia because in both cases people felt seen or observed. "His eye is on the sparrow," goes an old Gospel song, "and He's surely watching you." I like Freud's perception, but he forgot to mention a crucial distinction. In the case of the paranoid schizophrenic, the sense of being watched is almost always negative. In spiritual experience, it tends to be a heartening, comforting, or exciting gaze that wants to meet yours. That is the glance of the world that we have forgotten how to meet with a baby's undefended simplicity. We distrust everything, and sure enough, it won't talk to us.

"We are put on earth a little space," wrote William Blake, "that we may learn to bear the beams of love." These are not only sun beams or beams of light, but eye-beams, and they can indeed be hard to bear.

Why? If it is good, why do we find it too much? George Herbert turned aside when confronted by Love in his divine poem, "Love III", "Ah, my deare, I cannot looke on thee." But Love insists and keeps repeating the invitation, "Who made the eyes, but I?" until eventually, after many refusals, the shameful human puts his shame aside and accepts the gaze that Love has to offer.

It's reasonable for Rilke to say the torso looks at him without eyes since even in eye contact itself, the experience is not actually visual. It is not about me seeing your eyeball and you seeing mine. Often we can't recall the eye color of our dearest friends and intimates, because we are looking in their eyes, not at their eyes.

Sometimes, as a small child, Asher would get into a dreamy, prophetic state just before drifting off to sleep. One night in this condition he said,

> *Dad, everything looks the same. A truck, a banana, a hill.*
> *What?* I said, *Those things all look so different to me.*
> *No,* said Asher, *There's only one thing different:*
> *A human face.*

The very next night at bedtime he entered into that same dreamy state and he brought up the topic again.

> *Remember how I said everything is the same except a face?*
> *Yes,* I said.
> *Within the face,* said Asher, *it's the eyes.*
> And he was asleep.

Years ago at a conference led by Stephen and Ondrea Levine, we were all instructed to perform a Sufi exercise that involves a few moments of carefully orchestrated eye contact. You find a partner, hold their right hand with yours, place your left hand on your heart, and both of you turn in a single slow circle with eyes locked. I still use this exercise in many of my own groups, and it is always a risk, and a surprise, even a revelation, about the depths within the other person.

One of my partners at the Levine conference was a woman whose face was disfigured by extensive skin lesions. I was a little scared of her because she also wore an angry expression. As our eyes locked, everything around us melted away. We almost instantaneously entered and then passed through a succession of reciprocal roles. I was the compassionate

26

caregiver and she was a wounded bird. Then she was the big sister and I was a younger brother being instructed. I was her mother and she was my son. Then we were lovers, melting into each other. Then we were enemies, wary and plotting. Suddenly, all the roles crashed to the floor. What happened at that moment has stayed with me ever since. She and I disappeared as bodies, along with the entire visual field, so that now we were truly seeing each other. It is difficult to describe. We met in a shout of light.

E is for Eating. We all have challenges with food, it seems – taking in too much of it or not enough, or the wrong kinds. What, we might ask, is our real food? What really nourishes us?

There was a Swiss farmer in the 15th century, Niklaus von Flue, who wandered away from home, praying and confused. He didn't know where to turn. After a few days of sleeping out in the woods and the fields, he noticed that he had not eaten, and had no hunger. He went back to his village to ask a priest about it, and the priest said, "Eat when you get hungry." So he never ate again, and lived for 20 years, healthy, praying, focused on god. Contemplation was his meat and drink.

The "Lord's" Prayer (see *N is for Name* because it's not about a Lord) first has us ask for the intensification of being (which *is* the name in question), and then it soon moves on to eating. It says, "Give us this day our daily bread." The first meaning here can be physical; certainly we must help ourselves and others with physical food of all kinds. We live in a world with enormous and unnecessary hunger.

But "our daily bread" is probably a mistranslation. The kind of bread that is asked for is not "daily," which would in any case be a strange redundancy since it is already being asked for "this day." In the original Greek, it is called *epiousian* bread. "Give us this day our *epiousian* bread." Early commentators on the prayer went to the roots of this word, a rare term only used this one time in all of the Bible. *Epi* is "on" or "beyond," *ousia* is simply "being." So the sentence may actually mean, "Give us this day the bread of being." That's the recommended diet, both primal and ultimate. That was Niklaus von Flue's diet.

E is for Earth, and here is another open question: What does the Earth want? Instead of what we want to do with it or on it. Instead of even what the plant or animal or rock may want.

What does the Earth, Gaia, the Earth as a being, of which we are a part, desire?

Rilke had an answer. An intimate lover of land, water and sky, he wrote in the 9th of his "Duino Elegies" that the Earth wants to "arise within us invisible." And he immediately goes on to shout it out: "Earth! Invisible!" And then, as if repeating it in another form, "What do you want so urgently if not transformation?"

It would be hard to see what he is talking about, except that it goes along with our own clearest experiences, like the moment in the Sufi eye-contact exercise, when the reality and meaning of things makes them disappear as things. It goes along with the ancient, fragmentary Manichean texts that speak of the Terra Lucida or World of Light, Kabbalistic texts that speak of the broken vessels and their repair, apocalyptic texts that speak of the city of gold or transparent or white stone, and Buddhist texts like the Lotus Sutra where it is clear that the physical is no longer physical as we know it.

All these are realized in a kind of homeopathic dosage when-ever the world transmitted through the senses becomes touching or meaningful, and in that sense invisible, just as any text or utterance becomes invisible and inaudible to the degree that we are caught up in its meaning. At times of deep concentration, the sky or hillside, the stream or tree or herd, seem to come into their own at the same moment that we merge with them. Then they speak, wordlessly. The rightness of our dialogue with Earth also becomes apparent and transparent. "Now you've seen us," the objects on the beach seem to say to the young Ian McEwan in his reminiscence of a day on the Mediterranean (*J is for Joy*). They are no longer objects, then, standing outside him, but are inside and outside at once, like words we understand. The Earth is looking at him.

As we struggle with the day-to-day thinginess of our lives, as we notice the war of attrition waged against us by the meaningless parts of the man-made world and our own habits of thought and feeling and behavior, we can find an antidote in listening for the Earth's desire. We do this, once we know our own dignity and sovereignty, by allowing what is around us to have its own consciousness, its own sentient reality. What we notice soon enough is that Earth seems to want, not simply to be left alone, but to collaborate. Examples of this include the Findhorn community of the 1970's in Scotland and the still extant Kogis (*K is for Kogi*) of Colombia. Maybe Earth's ideal for itself is to become less of a planet shined on by an exterior sun, and more of a star among stars - green, blue, self-radiant. To find out, we can learn to let the Earth speak for itself, while recognizing that we are part of it, so that it *can* arise within us invisibly.

By the way, we know where the Earth is located in relation to the planets. And we know where our solar system is located in relation to the galaxy. We can even situate our galaxy within a vast multiplicity of other galaxies. We can see the expanses of space with our eyes and with extensions of our eyes. It's hard to locate the universe as a whole though. Where do you suppose the whole thing is?

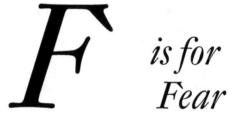

*is for
Fear*

*Crossing a bare common, in snow puddles, at twilight,
under a clouded sky, without having in my thoughts any
occurrence of special good fortune, I have enjoyed a perfect
exhilaration. I am glad to the brink of fear.*
Emerson, "Nature" 1836

The most common bits of reality – snow puddles, a bare field, a
cloudy sky – can fill us with such exhilaration that it takes us to
our limit and beyond, all the way to dread as Ralph Waldo
Emerson found. For behind all our normal fears of ill fortune,
of illness, of ill will, of loss and of pain, even the loss of human
life on Earth in its totality, there is a different kind of fear. We
just touched on it (*E is for Eyes*) with regard to the gaze of the
other. As a teacher of mine used to say, fear is an acronym,
F.E.A.R. It stands for, "Forever Evading Another Reality."

What is it, exactly, that keeps us from joyful acceptance when a
god or angel comes to visit?

*And they heard the voice of the LORD God walking in the
garden in the cool of the day: and Adam and his wife hid
themselves from the presence of the LORD God amongst
the trees of the garden…. And he said, I heard thy voice in
the garden, and I was afraid, because I was naked; and I
hid myself.*

> *And, lo, the angel of the Lord came upon them, and the glory of the Lord shone round about them: and they were sore afraid.*
> *And when I saw him, I fell at his feet as dead. And he laid his right hand upon me, saying unto me, Fear not: I am the first and the last.*

Adam, the shepherds, John – everyone is scared. Adam hides. The shepherds are "sore afraid." John falls down as dead.

I was particularly impressed by the encounter between Gabriel and the prophet Daniel, which I only stumbled upon recently:

> *Therefore I was left alone, and saw this great vision, and there remained no strength in me…. Yet heard I the voice of his words: and when I heard the voice of his words, then was I in a deep sleep on my face, and my face toward the ground. And, behold, an hand touched me, which set me upon my knees and upon the palms of my hands. And he said unto me, O Daniel, a man greatly beloved, understand the words that I speak unto thee, and stand upright: for unto thee am I now sent. And when he had spoken this word unto me, I stood trembling. Then said he unto me, Fear not, Daniel…*

Rilke talks about the disaster of meeting angels in his first "Duino Elegy." He calls them "nearly fatal birds of the soul," and says that if one of them actually heard his outcries and turned to address him, he would "die from its more powerful existence." This may be why in the Bible the angels often say, "Fear not," as, rather considerately, they seem to notice how overwhelmed we get in their presence. When they give a "Fear not" message, it seems to grant the human talking to them a temporary permission, like a passport, to live for a time in the direct laser beam of the angelic or divine love without getting vaporized.

Rilke also goes one step further. In a more obscure poem about the encounter of the Archangel Gabriel and Mary, he speculates that the angel was scared of the human, too: "They were both frightened" – not of something else, but of each other, of each other's gaze. The eye-to-eye connection got so intense that everything else disappeared around them.

Like Gabriel, we humans shudder not only when we meet a god, but also whenever we touch on the overwhelming reality of another human being. Our everyday fellow humans are sufficiently awesome or awe-ful. All it takes is a situation where we momentarily emerge from our perceptual ruts.

For instance, when you first meet someone, or when you say goodbye, there is a chance that the whole person will meet the whole person, and it will be like the moment in the movie *E. T. The Extra-Terrestrial* when the little boy and the alien first see each other and they both shriek and fall back in alarm. Maybe all social anxiety – the anxiety before a party, during a job interview, at a graduation, in lovemaking, in talking with someone who is near death – is originally and at its root a terror of the power and grandeur of the fact of the other person. We fear the implicit demand in it, the challenge, as George Oppen said of some deer he saw grazing, "that they are there."

I learned a piece of this when I worked as a waiter in my late teens. I saw how – and you must have seen things like this – when someone who had worked at the restaurant for a long time left the job, everyone lied about the loss of connection. They just lied. People would say, "See you soon," and "Don't be a stranger," and "I'll look you up if I ever get to San Francisco." Never did anyone say the obvious truth: "It's been great to know you here at this job. We almost certainly won't see or hear from one another again. Ever. This is the end of our relationship. Goodbye."

Strange to say, our persistent lie about people leaving the restaurant did not come from sorrow at the loss. We all pretended our way through the moment of separation whether the one leaving was beloved, or annoying, or totally indifferent to us. Leaning against a counter, drying a wineglass with a towel, I realized one day that it wasn't the fact that Fritz was leaving that made people cheerfully lie that they would see him again soon. Some were sorry to see the guy go, sure, but it was really a matter of downgrading the intensity of the moment of parting, when we slapped him on the back or evaded his eyes with a hug and a kiss. We were all busy diminishing the contact involved, pushing down the enormous hello that threatened to break through in the very midst of the goodbye.

I learned about the fear of meeting in another way when I met Mother Theresa in 1980. I had taken a year off after college and went to Calcutta, India to work in Kalighat, the Home for Dying Destitutes. I slept in a novitiate house in a Muslim quarter of the city. One day, I got to meet Mother T at her Mission House, 54A Lower Circular Road, in a little alcove to the side of the dining hall. She came across as highly self-aware during our talk. She wanted to know why I was there, and what I wanted, and what I wanted from her, and where I was housed, and what work I had already done with the Missionaries. As she listened to my answers, she kept saying, "Achaa, achaa" – the Bengali equivalent of "I see." She wasn't in a rush, but she wasn't going to waste time either. She was willing to listen and willing to speak, but above all she was willing to act. As we talked, I found myself scared of this tiny nun. It was not because she was famous or supposedly sacred. In person, she was a simple, overpowering deed. Like a hurricane. Mount Rainier. Genghis Khan. A calving iceberg. In her unostentatious, nearly silent way, she blew up my sense of what a human is. Just standing there.

For weeks to come in the food dispensaries, in the medical dispensaries, at Kalighat, in a nearby home for mentally handicapped indigents, I would be washing someone or carrying a load of supplies and Mother would suddenly be there working among us. Her mood, or rather her personal tone, was always pitched at the same sharp clarity. Filling a jar with water, righting the blanket over a sick child, nodding as she listened to a nun, spooning some rice and dal into a dying man's mouth, she gave the impression of a person so intentionally here, so deliberately a fact of the universe, that she could never not be.

When I lead groups, I sometimes ask people, "Why is it so hard to be loved?" Once a woman answered instantly and cannily, "It's destabilizing." We fend off the incoming light that could upset all our apple carts.

Jonah fled the being of being and hid in a ship, and later in the belly of a whale. Actually, what he fled was the compassion and the relatedness which flows from the heart of being. God had wanted him to get the wicked city of Nineveh to repent and become holy; Jonah was perfectly willing for the city to perish.

Eventually Jonah gave up, gave in, and accepted what he somehow knew he had to do. He preached then with his whole heart, and Nineveh was saved. He let in the light. Maybe we all can learn this turn, even after a lifetime of evasion. I think of my sister Abby who, when playing tag as a kid would eventually weary of flight, stop in her tracks, turn toward her pursuer, throw her arms wide, and cry out, "Have me in your clutches!"

G is for Give

My bounty is as boundless as the sea,
my love as deep; the more I give to thee,
the more I have, for both are infinite.
William Shakespeare, *Romeo and Juliet*

When I worked in Harlem Hospital, it was deeply moving to see the grandmothers and foster mothers who gave of themselves so endlessly for the sake of their kids with HIV and AIDS. They would haul the often reluctant children to every appointment, keep them on their medication schedules, feed them and try to get them into school and after-school programs, then tend to their bodies through horrifying opportunistic infections and other conditions, sitting up with them, racing them to the ER, handling their vomit and poop and blood, sharing their moans and the silence of their deaths, enduring beside them, then praying for them afterward. And it was all going on amid the noise, dirt, danger, delays, poverty, inadequate services and harassments that were a constant part of their experience. Rich in their connection to their children, the mothers kept giving.

Plants grow.
Animals move.
Humans give.

This sequence comes from Gitta Mallascz, who got it straight from heaven. It's not a hierarchy, exactly, but a sequence of appreciative characterizations.

The stone bones of the living Earth do get bigger at times by flow of sediment or lava, or by crystallization. Still, rocks don't grow and reproduce as plants do. Plants really grow.

Both rocks and plants move around at times. The boulder down the hill. The sunflower toward the sun. The shifting tectonic plates. Still, rocks and plants don't seem to move by any inner, conscious drive as animals do. Animals really move.

And all of creation gives itself. The whole thing is a gift. Still, humans are the creatives within creation whose individual, essential nature impels them intentionally to give. Even to give of their essence, to give more than is comfortable, to give what has never been given before through inventions of all kinds.

Mother Theresa used the phrase, "Give until it hurts." She didn't want rich businessmen to offer donations to her charities so relatively tiny that they meant nothing to the businessmen themselves. She wanted passionate, intense giving, just as she gave.

When I was four years old and we were living briefly in London, my mother (the maker of brass-rubbings with scary eyes) kept a journal for all three of us kids. She would sit at the manual typewriter every few nights and ask each of us for memories of our day. Then she assembled these into three separate diaries. Here's an entry from mine:

> *Jane had some bubble gum. She gave me a piece. I didn't ask for it or anything. She just handed it over.*

That miracle of unprompted giving still startles me. Of her own poetry, Emily Dickinson wrote, "This is my letter to the world, that never wrote to me." It is always a delight when someone I see in psychotherapy discovers what they want to give to the world, what letter they will write, even if the world never seems to write back.

At the other extreme, a patient often complains that his friends "owe" him phone calls, texts, emails: "He doesn't reach out to me." "They owe us a dinner." I tell him it is great to be the moon with its mysterious changes, its powerful, gentle radiance. Human moods can be like that in responding to the shine of others, similar to the moon reflecting the sun. But just as we need to see the sun more often than we need to see the moon, our stance in the world can become more solar than lunar.

To be solar is to shine whether or not someone else is shining on you. You make yourself a source. You take responsibility for starting the communication, or bringing the mood up. It's not about fairness. Don't wait for the other person. You start the good times.

Our abilities are themselves not solely of human creation. They are gifts given to us from who knows where and who knows how. The ability to give is a gift. We didn't invent it. Emerson: "The benefit outran the merit from the first day."

And the word "gift" in English does not originally designate a physical thing like a birthday present wrapped in a package. In its earliest usage, "gift" signified only a capacity or talent, like language, the ability to walk, to think, to feel, to see and hear. These are all capacities bestowed on us. Some people have special gifts, like a gift for music, or for political action, or for sports, or for gardening – superpowers. While these are learned activities in a way, there is no evidence that any human invented them as capacities. It is often clear to parents when a child has a particular gift from birth. The parents know it didn't come from them.

Philosophers sometimes call the total state of things "the Given." There is a world, an existence, given to us. Consider this:

> It's all I have to bring today—
> This, and my heart beside—
> This, and my heart, and all the fields—
> And all the meadows wide—
> Be sure you count—should I forget
> Some one the sum could tell—
> This, and my heart, and all the Bees
> Which in the Clover dwell.

Slyly and sublimely, Emily Dickinson begins without mention of what specific gift "this" is that she's bringing. Maybe the "this" of lines 2, 3 and 7 stands in for any "this" at all, or for the poem itself, her very act of utterance. She ends with a reference to being or bee-ing, a favorite pun of hers, since that is the greatest gift.

"This and my heart" is what Holly and I have inscribed inside our wedding rings along with the date. We've been bringing this this for forty years and more.

And G is for Gem. Consider that a normal pebble is opaque. We just see its outer face. A pane of clear glass, at the other end of the spectrum, is transparent. We see through to what's beyond it. A gem strikes the balance between these two. It is precious precisely because it is semi-transparent or semi-opaque. We neither stop at its outer face, as with a pebble, nor penetrate right through it, as with a clean window, but are drawn into a gazing that somewhat reveals its depths.

That's how it is with people, too. We can stop at their outer face, which includes what we like or dislike about them, their behavior, their self-presentation. If we do, they remain opaque.

Or we can overshoot and look all the way through to the simplicity of being itself that shines through them. Or we can see into them – in, in, in – where the depths, qualities and intrigue of life on Earth present a fiery bouquet.

H is for Hallelujah

We had friends whose son was named August. At age three, August used to appear at the top of the stairs each morning where he could see his mother sitting at the breakfast nook below.

"Mom!" he would cry out, standing there in his pajamas holding on to the railing of the staircase, his face aglow with happiness, "Great news!"

And she would look up from her toast, smiling, and ask, "What? What news? What is it, honey?"

But that was the whole story. There was no further content. He would patter down the stairs to join her at the table. His news was only the fundamental delight of the rising sun itself, leaping up within him. You could say, it was the great news that contains no information.

"Hallelujah!" he might just as well have said, and it would have been an accurate choice of words if he ever did. For the term *hallelujah* has two components, the *hallelu* part and the *jah*. The first means to sing out or trill out a song of praise. And the second part, *jah*, is short for the name of god, which is *Be*. (Again, *N is for Name*)

Hallelujah, in other words, means *trill of praise for being*.

That is what August did in his daily "Great news!" announcement. His gesture of praise was not about something else, but only about itself, about the thrilling announcement at the heart of things.

This *"Be"* book is a series of Hallelujahs, but now might be the moment to think about the *trill of praise* part. Why is it there in the word? Does god or the universe somehow need our praise, as if to have its narcissism stroked?

Why do birds greet the dawn? We so easily imagine the whole explanation is Darwinian, and that they sing only for utility, to attract a mate or to get food or to ward off danger. What if birds and humans greet the dawn not in response to it, and not with any practical use in sight, but as part of the fabric of the dawn itself?

The Greeks were aware of how numbers inhere in nature - as in the sequential chambers of the Nautilus shell or the whirl of pinecones. They felt the proportionality of things, and they sensed the divine in all the acts of nature. As a result, they called the whole world *beauty*, or *cosmos* in Greek (as in our word, "cosmetics"). They felt something about the totality that we totally miss. It would never occur to us to name the entire universe, "beauty." We have lost our sense for the gorgeous meaning which speaks as nature. The impulse to praise has been lost along with the perception of the world as a shower of blessings.

The expressive arts, like the universe as a whole, are useless in a certain sense. That is, they serve no practical purpose. Please don't think the arts exist in first order to investigate social norms, or to practice communication for the sake of later use at work or in personal relationships or in politics. The arts are ends in themselves. In this way they are worlds, self-justifying. You dance because you dance. They are neither contributions to nor adornments of the supposedly real business of getting stuff done. It is just the reverse: The practical things of life are there to support art, music, spiritual deeds of all kinds, generosity. To see this is to restore the universe to beauty.

I met an elderly Dutch man, the grandson of a blacksmith who lived in a tiny village toward the end of the 19th century. I asked him if he'd ever seen his grandfather at work in his smithy and if his grandfather sang while he worked.

"Oh, yes," he said. "Opa sang. In fact, he beat the iron on the anvil in time to the tune. And what struck me as a kid watching - that hammer was heavy, and the place was insanely hot. But at little moments when he held up the horseshoe or whatever to examine it, he kept right on singing and lifting that hammer up and down on the anvil to keep time."

So it wasn't that he sang to accompany his work. The song was the main thing and the work was the accompaniment.

My wife's paternal grandfather was known in the family as "Bigdad." He lived with his wife Deeda in Concord, Massachusetts for most of his long life, on a property with a swimmable pond. You walked from the house down a steep, fern-covered hill to the utterly secluded, spring-fed pond which was closely surrounded by woods. At the far end of the pond was a low bush that sported amazing purple flowers in Spring. One day we were down at the pond with Bigdad and I asked him about those flowers. He was in his 90's at that point and Deeda had died long before. He immediately identified the bush as a rhodora. He then launched into a recitation of Emerson's poem of the same name, including the lines,

> *Rhodora! if the sages ask thee why*
> *This charm is wasted on the earth and sky,*
> *Tell them, dear, that if eyes were made for seeing,*
> *Then beauty is its own excuse for Being;*
> *Why thou wert there, O rival of the rose!*
> *I never thought to ask; I never knew;*
> *But in my simple ignorance suppose*
> *The self-same power that brought me there, brought you.*

Even a rhodora that no one looks at, whose charm is wasted on the earth and sky, has a value or meaning, a self-same meaning. It means rhodora, and nothing else. It won't bend to our everyday sense of what needs to get done on our list of errands and goals.

Rhodoras are named for roses, though they aren't really roses. They are too original and uncultivated for that. But they share in what Andreas Schiffler, whose penname was "Silesian Angel," said about that emblematic flower:

> *The rose is without a why.*
> *She blooms because she blooms.*
> *She pays no heed to herself,*
> *nor cares if anyone sees her.*

I *is for Intensity*

The pervasive reluctance of young people today to actually speak on the telephone, like their preference for texting, seems to serve the function of delay or buffer. It is a way of avoiding the full blast, and the performance demand, of the social encounter. In Sherry Turkle's research a young person told her, "I'd rather text than talk." Turkle became aware of what she called "the desire to stay behind the safety of the screen and not expose themselves to the vulnerability of that face-to-face conversation, where things could go off on a tangent." So we're back to the realm of "Eyes" and "Fear," but this is more of a general trouble we all have with intensity.

Teenage and young adult patients of mine sometimes engage in self-cutting. They make cuts on their arms or legs or other body parts, frequently using razor blades. The intention is not suicidal, even though cuts are often on wrists and some are deep. Rather, they have described it to me as a self-soothing response to the anxiety of social intensity. A young woman festooned with tattoos and piercings explained that she went into the bathroom and cut her ankles only on visits to her parents' home when the psychic storm of family relationships became overwhelming to her.

T. S. Eliot said, "Human kind cannot bear very much reality."

Psychotherapists often encourage a person to relax or expand or just be honest in the face of emotional intensity. The goal is not to diminish the fearful emotion or event, but the opposite – to encounter it more consciously and skillfully. It might be a storm of rage, of fear, of sorrow, of jealousy, of shame, of confusion. One good reason to allow in more of these emotions is that then we do not have to obey them quite so much; we learn to live with them but not from them. The less tense, the more intense. We expend less of our energy trying to wall out and diminish what cannot be walled out in any case, and so we learn to meet and respond to it in its fullness.

This matters, because at the same time we avoid intensity in human encounters and in encounters of all kinds, we also long for it. The self-cutter may flee social interaction, but she is also very interested in the intensity of the moment: how deeply to cut, and the level of pain, and the likelihood of scars, for instance. Like any risk-taking behavior - gambling, parachuting, extreme sports, street racing – the high stakes are both feared and sought after.

Ramakrishna, the late 19th century Indian saint, was told by one of his educated disciples that there were tiny animals in every drop of pond water. He doubted it, so they brought in an ocular microscope, put some pond water on a slide, and showed him the amoebas and paramecia swimming in it. He was instantly catapulted into a state of overwhelming awe. He bathed in the glorious pervasiveness of life so deeply that he fell into a catatonic paralysis. They had to lift him from the chair and gently lay him on his bed and tend to him for a few days before he could return to normal consciousness.

Most of us don't have, and wouldn't want, disciples who will take care of us through days of unwavering astonishment. We don't aim to get destroyed by wonder. But we do want to go in the direction of Ramakrishna and still keep our day jobs. We want to open, as Emerson says, "at all risks, our human doors," and to turn our face to the faces of the world.

Faces? Yes, those sense-filled and intention-filled aspects that existence turns toward us when we turn toward them. The room I am in: I can sense into it using my imagination, perhaps with my body extended into a sphere that fills and embraces the room. The landscape: I can listen, look, be informed and also declare myself to it. Or there may be a sense of accompaniment by other presences. The spirit of the Earth, or a god, or energies, waves of presence. Other human beings are just one of the many intensities that we both flee and long to encounter. Let's not be too quick to limit the range or depth of our possible connections. Let's not be too quick to name them.

Only after years of practice in allowing intensities of being, of so-called things, and of invisible entities, did Rilke feel he could look at a curtain, a house, a lamp, and let them become, as he put it, "nearly a face."

I also stands for "I" – the self-designating personal pronoun of the subject. We're more alert to pronouns these days, certainly on college campuses, but they are mostly the third person ones such as *they, he, she, xie,* or whatever.

"I" is different. All other pronouns – even "we" – can be used by other people to sometimes designate you. The new concern about pronouns has to do just with this: anxiety about how others refer to you. But no one can say "I" to you and mean you. I is the ownmost, inmost pronoun that you pronounce only as and of yourself.

When you say "I", you perform I. You are "coming into being," in McEwan's phrase. You enact the very thing you announce by meaning it. "I" functions a bit like the word, "word," which both is a word and designates a word. By speaking "I," even inwardly and silently, you are the speaker incarnating the expression and the meaning of yourself in a single act.

The sense of the world's intensity and your own intensity grow together, as we have seen: new I, new world; new world, new I. As you open to intensities of all kinds, the so-called perceptual world may reveal itself as a face, an expressive face, that sees you I to I, without eyes. The world you thought you knew turns out to have been something like a scrim that concealed itself and, now that you are ready, reveals itself too. It is Elizabeth Bishop's "enormous morning, ponderous, meticulous."

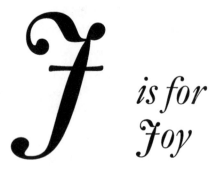

is for Joy

Joy... is the experience of reality.
Simone Weil

This alphabet-starting-with-B has a long background with other alphabets I have known. There were the sweet little alphabets of my grade school years that taught gender stereotypes, power relationships and a cutesy orientation to the animals we slaughter, and the agriculture we have mechanized and alienated. Those alphabets of indoctrination tended to have adorable pictures of boys in dungarees and checked shirts and girls in little frocks with their hair up in pony tails. The mommies and the daddies pictured, like the kids, were all white. The butterflies were oversized and round, and the trucks were small and comfy looking. These alphabets, like their implicit social messages, were absorbed and quickly forgotten. Only when revisiting such materials as a parent did I notice how much I liked the old books, but also how outdated, how thoughtlessly segregated and privileged they were.

A couple of alphabets with very different messages grabbed my attention in adulthood. The first was a book published as a benefit for AIDS research in which every letter was painted in a different, fanciful font by David Hockney. The editors offered one letter to each of 26 writers and celebrities, asking them to choose a single word that began with that letter and write about it. They gave "J" to Ian McEwan, and he made it about "an experience of joy, thirty seconds or so that I count as the real beginning of my conscious life." He tells the story of being left at the beach on the shore of the Mediterranean as a nine year old boy. He was alone, early in the morning with the whole day ahead:

> *The space which separated me from what I saw sparkled with significance. Everything I looked at - yesterday's footprints in the sand, an outcrop of rock, the wooden rail beneath my hand - seemed overpoweringly unique, etched in light, and somehow to be aware of itself, to 'know.' At the same time, everything belonged together, and that unity was knowing too and seemed to say, Now you've seen us. I felt myself dissolving into what I saw. I was no longer a son or a schoolboy or a Wolf Cub. And yet I felt my individuality intensely, as if for the first time. I was coming into being.*

I love this description of an unworried childhood moment in which, without distractions and games and screen-time, the boy comes to a very adult and, in fact, mystical level of realization. He finds joy in his relationship to nature – just as Wordsworth did when he referred to "the deep power of joy" in "Tintern Abbey." As with Wordsworth, the mood produced is both the cause and the result of altered perception in which we "see into the life of things."

McEwan has a feeling that what surrounds him is real, but more than that, that the world is conscious. It is not the familiar physical world any more, but has become aware, sentient, knowing, communicative, and continuous with the person beholding it.

Many years later, my friend Chris turned me on to the French philosopher, Gilles Deleuze (1925–1995). We started reading his impossible-to-read books. You wade into a Deleuze tome and for the first few pages you think, "Well, this is interesting. This is profound and suggestive. This stuff is cool." Then you start to bog down, as if your legs were in quick-setting concrete, or at least a hardening pudding. Every individual word looks normal, but the sentences no longer settle into any meaning at all. He seems to be writing from out of a field of reference, or maybe a dimension, that you cannot recognize.

Toward the end of his life Deleuze's student, Claire Parnet, convinced him that it was time finally to leave something on film for future folks to have easier access to his work. They came up with a film titled, *L'Abécédaire de Gilles Deleuze*, in which Parnet sits mostly just off-camera with Deleuze seated and talking. She pitches him each letter in turn and he extemporizes on a word it brings to mind for him. A is for Animal, and he has his own strange ideas there, praising ticks and lice, for instance. *Z is for zigzag*, the only way to go through life.

When it comes to "J," Deleuze picks "Joy" just as McEwan had done, and declares that joy is always delight in the exercise of a power. As he riffs and reflects and bounces around his topic, it's as if something is waiting for him and drawing him, and he eventually brings it out:

> *A typhoon is a power that rejoices in itself. It doesn't rejoice in destroying houses. It rejoices in being. To rejoice is to rejoice in being what one is, that is, in having arrived where one is.*

Again, nature is sentient and alive here, itself a physical trill of praise. Deleuze claimed he was an atheist. I'd say his thinking was not religious, but it was "grand, ungodly, godlike," as Melville said of Captain Ahab.

The teachers of religion, too, have emphasized joy. Teilhard de Chardin's words: "Joy is the infallible sign of the presence of God." It's not about the pleasure of having things go well – the perfect cup of coffee, or a good job, or many friends, wonderful as all these are. It's more like the in-spite-of-everything joy that I saw in the grandmothers of kids with AIDS in Harlem who could laugh and joke right in the midst of their endless, selfless caretaking of their mortally ill grandchildren. The joy of the Brothers and Sisters of Charity in Calcutta who were not brought down by their charges, but felt a deep, inexplicable, fundamental delight, awash in death and poverty.

I remember talking with a young Indian novice, a man in his early twenties who was in training to be a Missionary of Charity in Calcutta. We were comparing the different service possibilities: the roving medical cart that brought medicine to lepers throughout the slums; the rickshaws that picked up dying "untouchables" right off the street; the homes for the mentally handicapped; and the stations where they gave out food. I asked Brother Das where his favorite station was and he instantly answered, "Kalighat is my favorite place in the world." Kalighat is the Home for Dying Destitutes where Mother Theresa first began her mission to the poorest of the poor.

His answer initially took me aback. I had been white-knuckling my own brief service in those halls. After all, it was there that I wiped the poop off the behinds of shivering men, and doused the old ones with water as they sat screaming on the stone floor. There I had massaged the rash-covered limbs of men coughing up blood into little clay cups as they lay dying from TB. I had uselessly spooned rice and dal into the parched mouths of cachexic men who couldn't swallow and who then died the next day.

Yet the instant Brother Das mentioned his preference for Kalighat, I suddenly knew what he meant. Just there, where I turned TB positive from exposure to the bacillus, and caught dysentery that had me unable for weeks to lift my head or move off my own pallet, I had also felt a background joy I couldn't account for. Staring at Brother Das, I felt my preconceptions sliding away from me. "Yes," I said, "there is joy in Kalighat. In spite of everything. It is my favorite place, too."

The word "enjoy" has descended, as most words have, from an original height to its current low usage. When the word first came into English from French in the early Middle Ages, it actually meant "to render joyous." Like *enkindle* or *enliven* or *encourage*, to enjoy was an active, generative process. Over the centuries, the word has devolved to a passive taking of pleasure, as in, "I'll enjoy it if it's any good." We've lost both the challenge of the term and its empowerment. It's up to us to en-joy the day or the holiday, to bring and foment and be the joying of the moment.

The capacity to initiate joy lies within our zone of freedom. It's up to us to carry it out and perform it. In this, as in all giving, we are the inheritors, the heirs of, well, we can call it "god" or the "generative mystery" or the "source."

This is the kind of thing that whispered to the elders of Eastern Christianity when they came up with the phrase in the Nicene Creed in 325 AD that describes Jesus as "begotten, not made." It matters above all because we, too, are *begotten*, not made. Simone Weil pointed out, in her thinking about this theme, that whatever is made is always less than its maker. But heirs, begotten rather than made, can become creative themselves.

We have harmed our planet, in so many ways. An upside-down creativity. Now is the time for creative responses to our own self-made misery. They could include learning to perceive the expressive radiance of the natural world.

The old idea of "sons" as heirs to the "Father" has got to go. It's hopelessly mired in the sexist, patriarchal past. But the essence of it is not about male or female or other established categories. The essence of it is the inheritance of essence. We all have an ungendered, infinitely genderable and generous selfsame nature with the ultimate source. We are all royalty in disguise, gloomily unaware of our high birth - except for those moments when we wake and create. That is joy.

K *is for Kogi*

The Kogi of the northern Colombia coast live in a different world from ours: no electricity, no cell phones, no cars. They have only a slight connection to the modern world and its dubious conveniences. Around the edges though, they have come into contact with Spanish-speaking people and the technology outside their coastal mountain range. Reichl-Dolmatoff and other anthropologists have studied with them and learned their language and their ways. Some years ago, the Kogi noticed changes on their mountain peaks and wanted to send a message to the whole rest of the world to tell us to cut out whatever we are doing that is destroying the life of the planet. This is why they broke their centuries-long silence and isolation to collaborate with documentarian Alan Ereira for the film, *The Heart of the World*. They expected their message to be heard.

There are so many suggestive and challenging things about the Kogi, like the way they raise their ruler-priests in darkness. Selected at birth, certain babies are brought up in partial seclusion, fed a special diet, and allowed outside their darkened huts only on moonless nights. Older priests (mostly men, but all called "mamas") raise them, telling them the guiding myths and practices of a world they never see with their physical eyes until their coming-out ceremony at nine years old. When these priests-in-training emerge into the light on that day, they finally behold every butterfly, every twig and stone and person that has been described to them and placed in its mythic and spiritual context through all those years of darkness as the mamas talked and talked and talked. These strangely-raised, word-fed priests grow up to make every practical decision for the rest of the community. It is not that they have been raised without access to nature. They have been raised with access to nature as meaning – earth invisible.

The Kogi are an agricultural society, and the mamas decide which crops to plant in which fields, which new fields to make, which fields to leave fallow. This is neither a simple nor an arbitrary matter. The mamas put themselves into a meditative state, a collective mind they call aluna, and there they receive instruction from the spirits of the landscape and the grains. Then they plant the fields purely spiritually, purely inwardly, with the essence of those dictated grains. For a second planting, they imbue a few pebbles with the spirit of the specific grain for a given field, and bury these pebbles in the corners of the field. Finally, they instruct the farmers to plant the seeds of the physical grain – the third planting.

It would never occur to the Kogi just to plunk seeds crassly into the ground. They know that for the whole ecology of the mountain, there must be the initial deep listening, then these multiple plantings: one purely inward or mystical (in prayer), one shamanic or mythic (the pebbles), and one physical (with seeds). The visible, touchable world for them is only the final concretization of what is at root a communication among beings: the humans, the plants, the mountain itself.

Then, when the Kogi till one of those fields, treading back and forth in rows, it is for them the act of a god weaving one of the ritual shoulder bags the priests carry. Their every action, in other words, bursts with import and places them in a mythic context just as the stones are imbued with the spirit of the grain. In fact, they conceive of this planet as only one of nine levels of being, all of which interrelate and within which the mamas have their say and hold some sway.

And here's the amazing thing. It works. They kept their culture intact despite invasion and persecution by the Spanish. They have successfully cultivated the same isolated mountain range for many hundreds of years. All this is based on what Nobel laureate Barbara Ann McClintock called, "a feeling for the organism." They cultivate an intelligent feeling that grasps spiritual imperatives together with their practical applications as a single understanding.

We can't artificially jump into the consciousness of the Kogi mamas or the many others on the planet who still show traces of their primal roots. But the archaic cultures have a lot to teach us.

One feature is that they take terrestrial life seriously. The mythic context in which they set their every action does not render the physical world less precious or make it somehow illusory. No, they place the world within a vast cosmology, but this only makes the world entrusted to their care more real, more dear, more significant to them.

Second feature: the Kogi realize that the world cannot be managed from an alienated consciousness, unaware of its continuity with the sources of the world. They know that the planet is only liveable when perceived through more ecologically sensitive capacities. Developing and maintaining these capacities is worth lifetimes of specialized training. The Kogi are athletes of mind. They know that untrained, normal consciousness is simply too weak to endure and negotiate the desirous intensities of the whirling world.

K also stands for Know, Knowing. Our normal, everyday, educated, Western, Northern consciousness is valuable. It is a way of knowing that has given us the technology by which I'm typing and publishing these lines. It has given us the airplane, and steel, and electric light, and refrigeration, and reproducible music, and all kinds of positive goods and wonders. Yet this way of knowing, unbridled, looks to be ruining the whole planet.

Great teachers have challenged us to keep on knowing the world in the ways our culture suggests, but also to dare *not* to know anything, and so to take things a step further.

Seung Sahn, the Korean Zen master, lived by the slogan, "Only Don't Know." He meant, let go of the concepts – for instance, of the ego, the self, or of the so-called outer physical world, by which we typically understand and manipulate and dumb down all that surrounds us.

On the other hand, he also felt he knew, in some different sense of the word, the validity of that very statement, "Only don't know." So there is a knowing beyond not-knowing, and that's the interesting kind.

Or take Bodhidharma, the Indian monk who supposedly brought Chan Buddhism from India to China. (Chan is the originating tradition of Zen Buddhism in Japan.) When Bodhidharma was introduced to the Emperor Wu, the emperor asked him a good-student kind of question:

> *What is the highest meaning of the holy truths?*
> And Bodhidharma answered, *Empty. No holiness.*
> So the emperor, somewhat flustered, asked
> Bodhidharma, *Who are you?*
> To which the master said only, *Don't know.*

By saying the truth is empty, with no holiness, and he doesn't even know who he is, Bodhidharma was hoping to goose the emperor along, not into utter insensibility, but into a different kind of knowing, a different kind of holiness that has no recognizable qualities. He wanted Wu to arrive at the start of knowing, and not to settle for some specific bits of known content.

The knowing beyond knowing, the knowing that grasps nothing, appears and disappears in every culture. Whenever we encounter or experience it, it refreshes our take on the whole enterprise of living and dying and loving the Earth. Issa, a Japanese poet, also knew about letting go. He wrote a haiku on the death of his son that always draws me toward Asher:

> *Dew evaporates*
> *and all this world is dew.*
> *So dear, so fresh, so fleeting.*

Grab some river water in your fist and you have very little water. Leave your open hand in the flow, and the whole river is yours.

L *is for loss*

One loss, all loss, says Stephen Levine, author of Who Dies?, about how to approach death consciously. He knew that sometimes the fall of a leaf, observed by the open heart, or even just glancingly or casually observed, can haul you back in a whoosh to the death of a cousin, a friend – to the limitless ache. "All the new thinking is about loss," says Robert Hass, "In this it resembles all the old thinking."

Light or heavy, weeping or dry-eyed, and whether its about losing your job or a friend or a child, your own life or the life of the planet, there is a precious jewel to be found in the midst of ugly loss, the way the ancients thought there was a gem in the head of the ghastliest toad. Novalis, the German Romantic poet who lost his beloved fiancée Sophie when she was just 19, went half mad with grief. Yet he knew that it also brought him something immeasurably precious, and that his task was in some way to "keep the wound always open."

Because when something or someone matters to you enough, it forms an ineradicable part of the world you know. When that thing or that person is really gone in the form you knew, the universe breaks into smithereens, at least for a while. You yourself get shattered, since you and the world you know are one substance.

In that moment, or whenever the loss comes alive to you, it can be like the spiritual opening around a birth. What it is to be here, what "here" is, what "now" is, all undergo a shift. As you lose your normal footing, you become porous, out of your depth, beyond your own range, deranged, translucent. Right along with aching grief, unfamiliar winds of truth and light can blow clear through you. Rilke wrote about a friend's death, saying that it was as if she'd left the world's stage through an opening in the curtains:

> *And when you left, through that opening there gleamed onto the stage a beam of reality: green from the real green, real sunlight, real woods.*

For us, Asher's life was too short. Not long enough for him to teach us how to live so wisely and so goofily, so gratefully. I wish he were here now, as he was, making puns, surprising us with insights, or laughing with his brother. A few notes from a song like "Do You Realize?" by the Flaming Lips, will evoke him in an instant, and, in the same instant, the drop: he's gone.

At a certain point in sharing my grief over Asher's death with my friend David Spangler, a great teacher and a deeply empathic man, he nevertheless encouraged me to let Asher be on his way. David sees life on earth as cosmically important, but still not everything, and when it is done, the soul has other fish to fry. That particular performance is over. He's not sentimental about it.

Asher himself was ahead of the curve. At age five, he took a daffodil from the vase on the kitchen table to play with.

> Holly: *Put it back in the water, Asher! It needs the water to live.*
> Asher: *If I put it back, will it live forever? It will die eventually.*

And L is for Love. I woke recently from a dream unlike any other dream I've had. In the space in front of me hovered a face. It was the face of my wife's grandfather, Bigdad, who had died more than 20 years before.

Bigdad was a respected and beloved figure. A lanky 6'2" or so, he'd gone to Harvard, class of 1918. His sports were track and fencing. Served in both World Wars. Famously good marriage with Deeda, his wife of 50 years. Four children, all adorable and successful in various ways. Spent most of his life as a school teacher and principal.

Bigdad was courtly, with language that hearkened back to the 19th century in which he was born. He loved to sit out on the screen porch with a glass of sherry and talk about books or history or science or personalities. And he was eager to listen. He would ask searching questions and tend to be delighted with the answers, which made us all speak freely in his presence. He had his foibles, but as a host, a reader, a conversationalist, a giver of physical gifts, he had few peers. He never stopped learning. When he was 81 years old, my wife's step-father came out as transgendered. In those days, hardly anyone had heard of that category, but Bigdad's reaction was to research it, not to dismiss or condemn it. He realized right away that it was a variant of human experience that was new to him, and his love and concern for this in-law were unwavering. Bigdad was the one who recited Emerson's "Rhodora."

In the dream, Bigdad's face floated before me. As I looked, it started to dissolve into something coming from behind or within. This was love in a white light form. The face dissolved more and more, disappearing as the love grew more and more intense. The process came with a meaning: that this love is the substance of all that is. It was a love more total, more purely love, more radiant, more solid, than any love I had known, and in some way hard to describe or recall it was simply too much for me. Before Bigdad's face was quite gone, I couldn't hold it any more, and surged up out of sleep shaking, shuddering, convinced.

M *is for More*

In the Humphrey Bogart and Lauren Bacall movie, Key Largo (1948), the villain is played by the dastardly Edward G. Robinson. His character is named Rocco, and he is a thoroughly bad sort, a gin-running gangster and murderer.

At a crisis point in the film, while Rocco is holding the assembled company hostage, the father of the family, James, asks him what he wants, and Rocco hesitates. Frank, the Humphrey Bogart character, supplies the answer:

Frank: *He wants more. Don't you, Rocco?*
Rocco: *Yeah. That's it. More! That's right. I want more!*
James: *Will you ever get enough?*
Frank: *Will you, Rocco?*
Rocco: *Well, I never have. No, I guess I won't.*

The nature of attachment is precisely this: not to be satisfied. No matter how much Rocco gets, he will never have enough money, booze, gems, and so on.

It looks bad in Rocco, but the "more" orientation has something essentially human about it. Looked at from another angle, it is a magical element in our project of being.

In "Tintern Abbey," Wordsworth talks about experiences in nature that lighten the burdensome mystery "of all this unintelligible world." In feeling into the landscape around him, he is disturbed (*F is for Fear*) by the "joy of elevated thoughts," and he has a sense of "something far more deeply interfused." There's that more, but now it is part of an un-selfish project.

Skip forward a hundred years or so, head East, turn right after France, and proceed to the dying days of the Hapsburg Empire in Vienna. There we have Rainer Maria Rilke, who claims that everything around him, even things that have no name, is *closer*. The project of investigation involves an intensification that never ends.

The "more" of Wordsworth and the "closer" of Rilke refer to an inner self-increase. By investigating their own direct experience, they find a super-rational power of growth within the world itself, like Heraclitus' concept of the soul's *logos* or wording that increases itself.

When Paul Theroux visited France one time, he was asked by his publisher whom he might want to meet there and he instantly answered, "d'Aboville." Gerard d'Aboville had rowed solo across the Pacific, in part through life-threatening storms, over the course of four months. When Theroux met d'Aboville, he asked why he had undertaken such an arduous task. He said that he wanted to do more than just find the easiest way, the safest path through life:

> *I wanted to do something that was not useful - not like an animal at all. Something only a human being would do.*

This over-and-above-ness is the human quintessence at work. It looks beyond what is useful or efficient and adds an extra dollop, a potentially limitless perfecting with no final perfection in view.

Surprise is one of the hallmarks of the human "more." Surprise shows: there's more to your day than meets the eye.

I was giving a workshop on the campus of a home for mentally handicapped adults. The people who came for the workshop were so-called normal people, and I had normal conversations with them. Agreeable, normal. After a lunch break I happened to be alone, crossing an open commons, and a handicapped man a few hundred feet away started yelling at me and making aggressive gestures. Then he seemed to gather himself, tilted strangely, and set off at a run, lurching and lunging toward me, hunched over, still yelling with urgent aggression, and shaking his fist.

It was a scary moment. I didn't know whether to stand my ground and fight him, or just run. He looked small but was also wiry, his clothes in some disarray, and was obviously a man with the unconstrained fury of the mentally unhinged at his dispoal. Frozen to the spot, utterly unable to decide between flight and fight in the few seconds available to me, I suddenly realized it was too late: now he was upon me, rushing right up against me, his one fist raised to strike.

In a blink, everything changed. His yells or groans grew instantly soft as he gestured with his fisted hand into the crook of his other elbow to show me his treasure: a tiny bird he had found and carried nestled there in the folds of his jacket. That's all it had been about. "Look!" he said in gestures and gargled sound, "Will you look at this tiny bird?"

And M is for Meander. People in the business world like to quote Sun Tzu's, *The Art of War*, where he says, "Speed is the essence of war." It's about getting there first, getting your supply lines clear, the chain of command, instant fulfillment. Of course, there's a place for this.

But here is my corollary to round out a life: "Slowness is the essence of peace." If you want to make peace between yourself and your world, slow down.

A patient of mine, Paul, came in with a terminal illness and a concrete problem. He felt he couldn't get enough done in the little time he had. He was making himself sick with urgency: unable to really notice the roses he was supposedly smelling to check them off his bucket list. Traveling here and there, trying anxiously to say goodbye or at least connect with everyone, racing against his symptoms to fit in trips to museums and Broadway shows he'd never be able to see again.

I appreciated this anxious rush, having felt it myself with much less to justify it. I suggested he slow down, and wrote him a prescription. It read:

> *Linger*
> *Meander*
> *Ponder*
> *Saunter*
> *Savor*
> *Wander*
> *Wonder*

He took this medicine, and told me a few weeks later that he now needed less and less input to feel complete. Where he used to have to ski down a double black diamond, now he could be even more thrilled with the way the wind played over the uncut grass of a meadow. We speculated together what the limit was to this new skill: infinite delight in nothing at all?

Ellen Langer of Harvard reports, on the basis of repeated experiment, that we are happy in proportion to our noticing. The more things we notice, the happier we are. But we have to slow down to notice. How the coffee ring on the table makes a chubby hieroglyph. How the birds seem to chirp in unison, then in a kind of lop-sided call and response. The unique twist of a roadside retread. The maple tree's crazed bark.

The happiness we get from meandering and casually appreciating this and that along the way isn't an exclusively aesthetic experience or just a healing break from the woes and duties of real life. It's not only for our health, or as rest and relaxation, or to release endorphins and enkephalins in the brain, or to lower our cortisol levels. The pleasure we take precisely in the simplest word, thing, or glance is rather the beginning of the total miracle. "Look!" the children remind us, "Mom, Dad, look!"

N is for Name

The keynote prayer of Christianity is surely the "Our Father." After the opening salutation, its topic sentence, as my seventh grade teacher Mrs. Sharpe would have called it, boils down to "Hallowed be thy name," or in more common language, "May your name be made holy."

And, not strangely enough, one of the key prayers in Judaism is the Kaddish, an extended praise of "the Name," meaning again the name of god, urging it to be made holy and powerful.

What is this name that is so praiseworthy, and so important to be kept sacred?

In the Torah, the Hebrew Bible, by far the most frequently used name for god has just four letters, YHWH, or Yod-Heh-Vav-Heh. These are the four letters that are sometimes written out with vowels between them as "Jehovah" or "Yahweh" in English. Yet when Jews read the Torah out loud, we never say "Jehovah" or "Yahweh" or any other form of pronouncing those letters. Out of respect for the Name, when we come to this word in Hebrew, we mostly say, "Adonai" which means, "My Lord."

This particular name of god appears 7,000 or so times in the books of the Old Testament. In the English King James translation, as well as in subsequent versions, it is also not written out as YHWH, nor as "Jehovah" or "Yahweh" either. Instead, out of that same respect for the Name, the tradition is to write "the LORD," all in small capitals. "The LORD is my shepherd..." for instance. "The LORD spoke to Isaiah..." "Thus saith the LORD..."

7000 times.

YHWH, or rather its meaning, is the name that the Lord's Prayer wants to be kept sacred. And YHWH is the name that is praised so passionately in the Kaddish. And YHWH is what is really referred to by "in the name of Jesus," or "in the name of the Lord," or "in the name of Jesus Christ, our Lord." Because Jesus (incredible that this isn't more widely known) is just a form of Joshua, and means, "Jah saves" - Jah, once again, is short for YHWH.

So what, finally, does YHWH itself mean? What is its etymology? What does it signify?

Linguists who have studied the history of the Hebrew language agree that it means, in one way or another, (you guessed it) BE. That's the Name. And existence is its game.

This falls right in with the famous declaration from the burning bush in Exodus 3:13 and 3:14:

> *And Moses said unto God, Behold, when I come unto the children of Israel, and shall say unto them, The God of your fathers hath sent me unto you; and they shall say to me, What is his name? What shall I say unto them? And God said unto Moses, I AM THAT I AM: and he said, Thus shalt thou say unto the children of Israel, I AM hath sent me unto you.*

Now we are set up right, dear Reader, to re-read a lot of those hoary biblical passages.

It is not some male lord who is your shepherd, in the 23rd Psalm. "The LORD is my shepherd," means that Being itself, deeply felt, the creative primal urge, is my guide. This is not the day that some guy, some lord, has made, in the 118th Psalm, but, "This is the day that the drive to exist has made. We will rejoice and be glad in it."

The whole of the Old and New Testaments are invitations to an endless intensification of the sense of what is. An invitation to be here, on earth, now, rather than to go off to a distant heaven owned by a male deity.

And even if this program of intensification were not hidden in plain sight, pervading the Judeo-Christian tradition as it does all others, it would still be a good idea.

YHWH is such an ancient form of the verb, it is unclear what aspect of "be" it specifies. It may mean something like, "brings into existence." It may be the infinitive, the form of the verb that has no ending.

N is for Namaste.

When I took my first yoga class, the teacher and the long-term students all greeted each other and also said fairwell with the word, "Namaste." They folded their hands as if in prayer, bowed and intoned this Sanskrit term. The teacher told us that it means, "I greet the Divine within you."

I call it panning for gold. The miner who dips the pan in the river for gold is not shocked that the river is mostly mud. It's worth the hours and the back-breaking work for the rare glints of shiny metal here and there in the mess of river guck. "Namaste" reminds us not to bother too much with the apparent imperfections in the other person or in ourselves, but to focus on divine origins and essence.

"How often," Emerson says, "in my trivial conversation with my neighbor, do I notice that somewhat higher in us overlooks this byplay, and Jove nods to Jove from behind each of us." On another occasion he says, "Man does not represent himself, but misrepresents himself." And, "He is the façade of a temple in which all good and all truth abide."

So we almost have to look through and beyond what the other person is saying. As Louis Armstrong sang, "I see friends shaking hands, saying, 'How do you do?' They're really saying, 'I love you.'" There's the message, and then there's the meta-message.

Another way of saying "the divine" in the other person is "the positive possibility." Buried in everyone is a possibility for change and creativity. This makes all the difference, and keeps us, in William James's term, from too swiftly closing our accounts with reality. There is always more in the other person, as in oneself, and that is why every judgment of another person is invalid and partial. Even if I correctly condemn certain behavior, even if I decide, for instance, that it is bad idea to hire or marry someone with a given past and a given present, we know this is an incomplete gesture as far as a full appreciation of that human life. The embers of possibility may still be there smoldering faintly underneath no matter how many layers of ash.

I was driving one day with the five-year-old Asher and we saw a billboard, a public service announcement against drunk driving. It showed crash dummies smashing through a windshield and the caption was something like, "Don't be a dummy. Don't drink and drive."

Asher pointed at the billboard and said:

> *I know what those are.*
> ML: *What are they?*
> Asher: *Action figures!*
> ML: [I explained about crash dummies and their use in testing car safety to approximate effects on human bodies.]
> Asher: *Why don't they just use villains?*
> ML: *Wow. Well, even if someone has done something very bad, there is mostly still some good in them, a divinie spark. So you can't use a human being as a crash dummy. You want to find the good in them.*
> Asher: *What if someone is all bad?*
> ML: *Um. Maybe some people are all bad, but it is just very hard to tell.*
> Asher: *OK, Dad.*

And N is for No. Not. Nothing.
In Ian Hamilton's biography of Robert Lowell, he recounts how for a later edition of his poems, Lowell added "not" to

various lines. If the line had been, "It was raining that April day," Lowell might change it to, "It was not raining that April day." His editor at Farrar, Straus wanted to know the facts, these being famously confessional and biographical poems. Was it raining or wasn't it on that April day? Lowell simply said that it was more interesting with a "not."

The question, "Why is there something rather than nothing?" does require some friendliness with "nothing." *Nothing* is itself a positive resource, a weighty treasure, one of the most important things there is, or rather isn't.

It is against the stark background of a possible nothing that we appreciate the actual, factual hereness of existence. This floor, for instance, that might not be there, but is. Nothing makes something pop.

Elizabeth Bishop discovered this while listening to her aunt's moan of pain in the dentist chair, a moan with a distinct duration and quality, a cry of pain that could have gotten louder, for instance, but didn't: "How – I didn't know any other word for it – how 'unlikely.'"

Look around you. All this world – and all its history – could perfectly well not be here, but it just is here. *How unlikely.*

Death, too, because of its not-ness, is a goad to an appreciation of the real. It is the apparent nothing and nowhere of death – a radical otherness – that makes us marvel at the weird situation we're in here on Earth.

John Keats wrote:

> *When I have fears that I might cease to be*
> *Before my pen has gleaned my teeming brain*
> ....

then on the shore
Of the wide world I stand alone and think
Til love and fame to nothingness do sink.

Keats died young, and knew he was terminally ill with tuberculosis when he wrote that poem. He'd already seen two of his brothers die. Instead of shying away from death, which would leave it opaque, or looking beyond death to a heaven which would render it transparent, he was willing to look into death's gem, into the no, not, nothing. Projects will go unfinished. He will never marry. He doesn't cheapen the experience by saying what exactly he thinks, which wouldn't be in normal words and concepts anyway. It was nothing, too.

Let's thank the possibility of non-being for its help in marveling at the non-thing-like reality of all that is. Let's put our hands together, bow low, and say, "Namaste, Nothing! I greet the divine within you."

Another time, an early-grade-school Asher and I were sitting and watching a cloudless Saturday morning come in through the window. Out of the blue he commented:

> Asher: *Daddy, there can't be a beginning to everything.*
> ML: *Why not?*
> Asher: *Because whatever you said was the beginning, I could say, 'What came before that'?*
> ML: *That's so true. Still, what if there was something that had its own start inside itself, so you didn't have to go behind it to see what came before?*
> Asher (narrowing his eyes): *That wouldn't be a normal thing at all.*
> ML: *But it wouldn't be nothing…*
> Asher (eyes wide, suddenly aglow): *I know what kind of nothing that would be!*

O *is for Open*

When Asher's younger brother Rody was little, we were driving to the house of our friends, the Sagarins. The conversation went something like this:

> Rody: *We're going to the school.*
> ML: *No, we're headed to the Sagarins' for lunch.*
> Rody: *This is the way to school. We're going to the school.*
> ML: *Yes, for most of the way it's the same, but at a certain point we won't turn right, we'll go straight, because the Sagarins live near the school, but actually on a different road.*
> Rody: *We're going to the school.*
> ML: *You'll see.*
> Rody: (singing out, delighted, at the moment we failed to make that right turn to the school):
> *I was wrong!*

And I thought, "Boy, do we ever lose that." The delight in being wrong is just one of the treasures of openness that childhood shows. A freedom from prejudice, from habit, from clutching, from the self-protective self.

A Black friend in Harlem raised two daughters. An older cousin of theirs had married a white man, whom they knew as Uncle George. One time at a family reunion picnic on the beach, the girls (aged seven and nine) saw him flipping burgers and suddenly noticed, "Uncle George! Uncle George! You're white!" Uncle George replied, "Yes. That's a fact."

What had he been to them before? Well, he had been what he beamed at them. Uncle George, a kindly voice, the offer of another burger or piece of cake, a radiant smile. He hadn't previously coalesced into *white*.

I was ten or eleven and sitting in a dentist's chair in New Haven, not far away from Elizabeth Bishop's in Worcester. The assistant wheeled over part of a machine I hadn't noticed before, and guided a blue metal cone toward me with its blunt point aimed at my jaw line.

Assistant: *We're taking a picture of the inside of your mouth.*
ML: *How can it take a picture? There's no lens!*
Assistant: *It's an X-ray machine. It can see through the casing.*
ML [all mystery gone]: *Oh, OK.*

This is the fall of man. In an instant, the openness (*It looks through the casing?*) was gone. At her word "X-ray," I replaced my wonder with a weak substitute concept, a sort of pseudo-concept that was already familiar to me from Superman comic books and TV shows. The marvel was gone and Marvel Comix (*X-ray vision!*) took its place.

It's not a given that we will reconstitute our early childhood openness in adulthood. It takes some doing on our part. A friend used to say that the best line in the New Testament was, "Behold, I make all things new." How?

One of the best methods I've found for re-opening our hearts, and so making the world new, was mentioned in a talk given by Rachel Naomi Remen. She calls it, "Growing new eyes." I've somewhat expanded it over the years.

I call it by the acronym STIGA. It stands for:

> *Surprised*
> *Touched*
> *Inspired*
> *Grateful*
> *Amused*

Surprised is surprised. What surprised me today? You think of it, notice it, turn your mind back to it. I was surprised this morning, for instance, when a deer shot past me, swerving millimeters away from my car as I drove into the office.

Touched. What touched me? Where surprise can be negative or neutral, being touched tends upward. For example, I was touched by a visiting child's eagerness to play Jenga with another child she'd just met at our kitchen table. Her good will, her readiness, her freshness, her attack of the game!

Inspired. This isn't about motivation. It's not, inspired to *do* x, y or z. It's about inspiration in the sense of realizing there's more that is wonderful in the world than you previously thought. Marveling, amazed, in wonder, in awe - that kind of thing. This morning I was inspired by the thought of a patient of mine who makes his own ukeleles from scratch. As he talked about it, I was in awe of the care and precision he brought to bear on the task.

Grateful. Leaving the house early this morning, I was so grateful for the chairs Holly got for our kitchen. We'd suffered with the same antique chairs for two decades as their joints continued to loosen and crack. She finally just insisted, selected, ordered and *poof* – we have these great new chairs. Thanks, Sweetheart!

Amused. Everyday in my work I find that I both laugh and cry with my patients. Tearing up with a patient is a more famous category, and in some ways more professionally acceptable than laughter. Just yesterday, I was talking about a serious matter with a patient when he made a Freudian slip that was so obviously significant and sexual, we both burst out laughing.

When remembering or writing down these moments in your day, you can resolve to be again surprised, again touched, again inspired, and so on by the events in question. Even though you might think it is impossible to be surprised again, and to be even more strongly surprised, by something you already know about, it can be done. By turning the events over in your mind a little, by approaching them afresh, you can intensify the original experience.

Practicing any version of this exercise repeatedly, over weeks and months and years, it slowly turns your emotional life outward and upward.

Outward: Anger, fear, jealousy, humiliation, are occasioned by the outer world to some extent, but the main focus in negative emotions is on oneself, one's inner state. With *STIGA* and its relatives, the main focus is outside yourself. You train your feeling-sensitivity to sense the world and its qualities with more depth and variegation, rather than just your own inner weather.

Upward: The *STIGA* practices turn your emotions toward the good. After *Surprised*, they all focus on various kinds of positive experience. You'll spend less time on what is hateful and impossible, more time on what is lovable and doable.

You, dear Reader, are the one who can make all things new. Then you'll find yourself looking at life both from far off as if through a telescope, and from up close as if through a microscope. And without special instruments, too, you will be astonished at how it all just is.

P *is for Pour*

The laws of the natural world as described by physics don't actually keep the universe going. Or, they keep things going within the physical world as normally assumed. They don't solve the root issue of existence in the slightest because, like everything else, the laws of physics – which are real – might be there or might not be, moment by moment. They can't account for their own origin, or for why there would be a Big Bang and what came "before" it. And they can't account for their own continued relevance at any given moment. And they are not the only way of looking at the world.

I recognize the validity and importance of scientific investigations: not doubting climate change or evolution here! We need science and technology (and a total change of heart) to help us address the mess we've gotten ourselves into through science and technology -- and the greedy heart. Still, physics has theology-envy: it wants to say it accounts for everything when it only accounts for what takes place within itself. Physicists I have known are profound and wonderful beings, and many of them still marvel at the abiding impossible question: what makes the *whole thing start* and *now continue*?

The hum of reality keeps humming. Chairs, walls, people, trees and the laws of thermodynamics, all subsist and exist and persist.

The origin of the word "god" in English, as in other Germanic languages, is an Indo-European root that means, "to pour." It may have originally meant the pouring of oil on a statue, or the pouring of wine on the earth to bless it, but I prefer to think of it as an overflowing fountain. God, the origin of the word itself seems to want us to know, is the gushing forth of all that is and can be, and we are part of it. Something or someone – or even a source prior to the distinction between *what* and *who* – poured forth a universe and now keeps on pouring.

The dogwood pours out its cheerful blooms. The birds return in Spring. The stars shed light quietly, mostly invisibly, around the clock. Just as these things keep giving of themselves, our minds are constantly renewed. We keep having fresh perceptions, fresh ideas - however sparsely sprinkled in among the tons of stale old ones. Keats knew that real intuitions come to us "as easily as leaves to a tree." Everything keeps arriving that way.

And you yourself are not a ready-made item given by fate or god. Recall those lines Shakepeare's Juliet spoke that kicked off *G is for Give*:

> *My bounty is as boundless as the sea,*
> *my love as deep; the more I give to thee,*
> *the more I have.*

The more you give, the more you have and then, the more you are. Rather than a fixed set of characteristics, you are a self-creating, self-intensifying source, a melody improvising itself just now.

 *is for Question*

When Gertrude Stein went back to visit America from her adopted home in Paris, she was asked to sit in and lead a graduate philosophy seminar at Harvard for the day. It went well, and following the luncheon she talked with the professor who normally taught that class. It was a graduate student in philosophy at Princeton who told me about their dialogue, which I recall like this:

> Professor: *Well, Miss Stein, the students were more talkative with you than they normally are with me. I suppose it's because your reputation preceded you.*
> Stein: *That's not why.*
> Professor: *What? Well, if not that, then why do you say they were more talkative?*
> Stein: *You see, when I ask a question, I don't know the answer.*

Teachers mostly ask questions to which they already know the answer all too well. It has a deadening effect. "What's 35 divided by 7?" asked Mrs. Salowitz in 4th grade. The class fell into three groups. Those who didn't care. Those who didn't know but still feared to be called on. Those who knew the answer and threw up their hands, waving them until they had to support the upheld arm at its elbow with the other hand. But everyone knew there was no real question at stake.

A real question doesn't already have an answer. It troubles you as the full moon troubles the cat, and sets you on a quest. It may turn out that the seeking itself, and the adventures along the way, are more important than any result. That's the point of C. P. Cavafy's poem, "Ithaka" (but also of everything else). "When you set out for Ithaka," he writes, "ask that your way be long, filled with adventures, filled with surprises."

What is this world? How can I know it more intimately? How can I contribute my share? Who are my people? What's the best we can do with this mess? These are real questions because they matter to me, and I don't know the answers.

It's a welcome partial satisfaction when such questions, which can never even be asked in final form, do somehow receive provisional concrete answers. This happens by asking them sincerely. I try not to swerve aside from the partial answers that come, even when they seem cliché, as long as, for me, they carry the whiff of reality. And I notice how partial they are, sometimes making me realize the question has just changed in the answering and the answer that comes is to a better question that I hadn't quite asked yet.

Here are some examples:

> This world is one in which growth happens at the boundaries, as languages intermingle in port towns and cities grow at the intersections of rivers, or new ideas pop up in lively conversation between people of different views and backgrounds.

> You know the planet more intimately because age is making you slow down. And a strange accretion is happening, a thickening as of a béchamel or a balsamic reduction, whenever you pause and notice.

You contribute by doing what you are good at, not by straining.

You know by a kind of instinct who your people are as they arrive. You ache when they leave.

We'll manage this mess collaboratively or not at all. So maybe not at all.

What are the questions, dear Reader, that matter to you? Will you take a stab at provisional answers? Any question real enough to matter, asked with a willingness both to not know and to know, will draw other meanings and sensations along with it. The hummingbird's hollow bones will lead on to the mysterious iridescence of its throat feathers. A cloud of realizations accompanies the arrival even of the inadequate answer.

When Gertrude Stein lay dying, a friend at her bedside, assuming that Stein's perch at the boundary would unveil an ultimate secret, asked her, "What is the answer?" To which Stein replied, "What is the question?" and died.

R is for Real

Here in the Berkshires, Holly has a garden – a real garden. In it, we smell the heavenly tomato plants. We hear the buzz of mosquitoes and feel their sting. We open the peapods with a fingernail, and munch on the line of green little globes in the full summer sun. Sometimes we hear the rustle of a toad and see it scootch along, seeking shade. Our senses help us to feel into the real, even if our gaze stops too soon, too superficially satisfied.

That overall sense for the reality of the garden, as we saw in "C is for Can," has been taken as a criterion of mental health. But the reality of the world as we perceive it is fundamentally questioned, even denied by natural science itself - the very science that gives us psychiatric texts like the *DSM-V* and the *ICD-10*. Physics seems to show that our everyday world, our lived experience, is an illusion, and what is "really" there are tiny charges of electricity or other forces or potentials with vast spaces between them. We only perceive these things as the objects and persons of our normal experience because of how our senses are constituted.

So what is reality? Is it the world of normal experience, or some intensified version of it, or the world of particles and forces, or what?

It's helpful to think of Marianne Moore's definition of poetry. She called poems "imaginary gardens with real toads in them." Real toads like anger or greed or despair. Moore's idea takes us outside of both our normal sense perception and the minutia of physics, to an exact sensing of the real as *meaning*. What is real for me is what signifies to me: like the anger or misery or joy a poem expresses.

We can consider an old Hasidic tale here. The story goes that a rabbi and his son are sitting on the stoop of their apartment building. A man walks by in his long gown and fur hat, greets the rabbi, and says,

> *Rebbe, I'm about to get married, but I'm a few kopeks shy of payment for the wedding feast. Can you loan me a little something?*

The rabbi reaches out with his walking stick and parts the man's overcoat to reveal that inside he is wrapped in his funeral shroud. *Be off! he says, You're dead!* And the man vanishes into thin air.

The boy turns to his father in some astonishment and asks, *What was that?*

Oh, says his father, *that was a man who had died, but he was wandering in a place of confusion. He told himself this story about going to his wedding feast. I just had to remind him where he was, and he could go on with his journey after death.*

How do we know, asks the bright boy, *that we are not wandering in a place of confusion ourselves, right now?*

The place from which you ask that question, replies his father, *is the real place.*

As Simone Weil reflected: "It is given to very few spirits to know that things and beings exist."

In the context of her letters and essays, Weil seems to mean that we don't fully know either normal sensual or consensual reality, nor the truths of physics, nor the reality of the toad in the poem, nor the real place of the boy's questioning - unless we develop a special kind of attention.

Dreams can be a model for this special attention. With normal human dreams, we only know about the dream afterward. That is, we dream at night, but in a semi-conscious state so that we become fully aware of the dream, able to think about it and know it is a dream, only after we wake up and remember it. A dream we can consciously think about is a remembered dream. That's normal dreaming.

We all go into REM several times a night without waking, and recall our normal dreams only if, through intervention or by natural means, we wake right out of a period of REM. So most dreams go un-remembered. They swim past us in a silent, unexperienced invisibility like schools of fish, too deep even to guess at, under the night river's black and endless current.

Even remembered dreams are only partially recalled, and then so easily forgotten. Have you ever wished, not only to be able to remember a dream on waking, all so misty and fragmentary, but to become more aware within the dream itself? To know it during its very course?

You can, in fact, wake up to consciousness within your dream in what is called lucid dreaming. The waking self, your normal daytime self, realizes in a flash that you are in a dream right then, while the dream is still progressing. Often it is an anomaly within the dream story, a weird event or situation that cues you to wake up while the dream is still flowing.

"That's a funny kind of table," you might say to yourself in a normal dream. "It has hair and it's singing." But in a lucid dream, you might go on to say, "Wait a minute. There is no such thing as a hairy, singing table. Oh! I see. This is a dream! This table, these people, are all dream figures. I'm awake now inside my dream!" It requires a special second glance at what is around you to enter lucidity.

Such a moment comes rarely for most of us, and it's striking when it does. It is not merely a "false awakening," that much more common experience in which you may dream about waking up in bed but then later you really waken and realize you had a dream of waking up. No, this is you, the fully conscious you, waking up fully, in the midst of a dream world.

You can know it is your waking self and that you are truly awake within the dream because often the experience is so exciting, so interesting, that you only manage to continue to dream in this lucid way for a few moments. The very thrill of attaining lucidity shakes you out of REM, and you find yourself opening your eyes in your bed, wishing the dream had continued. This waking-directly-from-the-lucid-dream allows you to feel the continuity of your consciousness within the dream and your consciousness now that you have opened your eyes in the bed. Like rising out of snorkeling: the same person who was looking at the fish and coral below seamlessly rises to look at the shore, the boat, the sky, the other swimmers.

Now, finally, the point of my analogy. What I'm always talking about as the direct experience of being is much like a moment of lucidity in a dream. You awaken within this life into a stronger awareness of your actual situation. You look around and say, "Oh, this is life. This is happening. This is the universe. Now I see clearly what all along I've been dozing through."

There's a difference though. In lucid dreaming, we wake up within a dream world and see its unreality. In the direct experience of being, we wake up within this world and see its reality for the first time.

> *We are such stuff as dreams are made on, and our little life is rounded with a sleep.*
> Wiliam Shakespeare

S is for Surface

In high school, a friend was puzzling over a rock. He had been turning the rock over in his hands and wondering what it looked like on the inside. Then he smashed the rock with a hammer and it broke in half. On the broken halves he saw sparkles of quartz exposed to the sun.

OK, he thought, but these crystals are now on the *surface* of the two halves of the rock. I am not looking *inside*. I have only made a new surface. Even if I drilled a hole and put a tiny scope into the center of the unbroken stone, when I looked through it what I'd see would be surface for me. I can never look *inside*.

The stunning experience of being is not an experience of something hidden and mysterious. Rather, like the inside of a rock, it is hidden and mysterious until revealed. So it is an experience of unusual openness and evidence. Everything has become clear. As in waking from a dream but within the dream, you feel that you didn't understand your real situation until now. It doesn't demote the previous moments to unreality – just the reverse. It makes you see how very real all that you previously thought was real really is.

Sometimes we think of religion, spirituality, and so forth as an endless mystery. With regard to all kinds of ultimate things, such as the afterlife, people often say, "We'll never know." It is easier to leave ultimate things hidden and shrouded - similar to the way Churchill characterized the possible actions of Russia as "a riddle wrapped in a mystery inside an enigma."

Spiritual teachers of all traditions have challenged us in the opposite direction, asserting that we will all eventually know every essential thing. We do look into the entrancing depths of a gem (*G is for Gem* as well as for *Give*), but the fate of our mysterious world is to become less mysterious, more available to us than it now seems, and in this sense more surface.

This may be what it means that Jesus walked on (the surface of) water, and is certainly why he said,

> *For nothing is secret, that shall not be made manifest; neither any thing hid, that shall not be known and come abroad.* Luke 8:17

What is translated here as "come abroad" is the word *phaneros* in Greek which really means, "apparent, clear, visible, manifest" according to *Strong's Greek Dictionary of the Bible*, and also meaning "light," as in bringing things into the light so that they become visible.

This everything-must-show attitude is behind Paul saying,

> *But God hath revealed them unto us by his Spirit: for the Spirit searcheth all things, yea, the deep things of God.* 1 Corinthians 2:10

And this is why the prophet Jeremiah reported:

> *After those days, saith the LORD, I will put my law in their inward parts, and write it in their hearts; and will be*
t > *their God, and they shall be my people. And they shall teach no more every man his neighbour, and every man his brother, saying, Know the LORD: for they shall all know me, from the least of them unto the greatest of them.* Jeremiah 31:33-34

And this is why Zen master Dogen asked the cook:

> *What is the practice of the Way?*

and the cook responded:

> *Nothing in the whole world is hidden.*

Dogen, Instructions to the Cook, c. 1245

And, this is why we have the Islamic tale of god giving the reason for creating a universe with humans in it:

> *I was a hidden treasure; I longed to be known.*

And S is for Substance. When I was about 14, I might well have said if asked about the nature of the world, "Well, the actual substance of the world is matter."

The word *sub-stance*, as we have all forgotten, is the Latinate version of *under-standing*. It originally referred to meaning and to makers of meaning. Radiant meaning (which is understood, or it isn't meaning at all) is the very substance of the world. The word *sostanza* in Italian would be used as late as Dante to mean angels. And what of *matter*? It originally meant *mother*, and has gone through the same descent as so many other words.

So instead of saying, "The substance of the world is matter," it might be better and more accurate, but very unlike my 14-year old self, to go to the roots and to say, and to mean, "The angel of this world is the Mother."

These words, *substance* and *matter* could remind us to feel into the ways in which the Earth, traditionally a female deity named Gaia, is a being who both holds us and permeates us. She is, perhaps, the spirit referred to by Wordsworth in "Tintern Abbey":

> *…and I have felt*
> *a presence that disturbs me with the joy*
> *of elevated thoughts, a sense sublime,*
> *of something far more deeply interfused,*
> *whose dwelling is the light of setting suns*

and the round ocean and the living air
and the blue sky, and in the mind of man,
A motion and a spirit that impels
All thinking things, all objects of all thought,
and rolls through all things.

Wordsworth saw into the life of things. He was himself alive in a breathing, substantial world – not a world of matter but a world that matters.

T is for *Task*

A lot of freebies come toward you when you practice attention and concentration.

One freebie is calm. In the moments of absorption, you have no other concerns, so the real care-freeness is automatically there. You become all rock, like Barbara Ann McClintock, the Nobel laureate in biology who forgot her name while writing an exam essay in geology. As soon as one leaves absorption, of course, the standard self and its worries come roaring back. She remembered her name after a few minutes of sitting there in the exam room, but never lost the trick of total immersion.

Another gift is adaptability. You, or the day around you, start to free up, and be able to swivel in any direction. The moment becomes what is called in mechanics a "universal joint." You come unstuck.
The most potent of the gifts that come with absorption is the sense of task.

This is what Rainer Maria Rilke experienced that day while looking at the broken marble torso of the Greek god, Apollo. (*E is for Eyes*)

He described for us the gleam of the statue's eyes that had sunk down into the body itself. The headless form is looking at him. Every spot on it is aglow with gaze. Then there's a break in the text and with no connecting explanation the poem ends:

> *You must change your life.*

Rilke's careful study of the statue had turned into an impulse directed from the statue to him, a jolt. He gives us no specific content to the change demanded of him. It may have been something specific, like taking his work more seriously, or traveling to Russia. I think, instead, that it gave him the absolute and fundamental inspiration.

U is for Un-graspable

We were driving through a dicey part of Brooklyn one day and Asher called out from his car seat in the back.

> Asher: *Daddy, is god a person or a feeling?*
> ML: *What do you mean?*
> Asher: *Like a person you could talk to, or a feeling like peace or love?* [As a trained Clinical Psychologist, I knew my best move here was evasion.]
> ML: *Good question. What do you think?*
> Asher: *I think it's like chocolate in your mouth.*
> ML: *How is that?*
> Asher: *You know how a square of chocolate in your mouth is hard at the center, but then it melts around the edges and turns liquid after a while?*
> ML: *Yes. But how is god like that?*
> Asher: *At the center is a wise being, and it turns into love all around.*

If we put any serious time into amazement, it turns into love. Being turns into love as we savor the ways of the world: the fact of the other person, for instance, or the fact of the traffic light as well as the crashing surf. By holding the world in our mouth until it melts.

This kind of experience is available – and ungraspable. We have an insight, a flash of light, an access to intimacy or meaning that seems eternal, but these intensities of being are hard to locate and, once found, they are already far off again, fading away mysteriously like the Grail Castle.

In Wolfram von Eschenbach's early telling of that tale about a thousand years ago, the young Parzival finds his way to the Grail Castle, sees the Grail King who is horribly wounded, and experiences something of the generosity of the Grail itself. The glimpse is not his to keep. As he watches, it fades like a dream, and the very tracks of the Grail-bearers' horses are magically erased from the road.

This tale corresponds to our sense of the sacred moment as fleeting and already gone. Sometimes we push off the sacred into the future, instead of into a fading past. With the idea of the second coming of Christ, the Maitreya Buddha, the Green Man of Iranian Sufism, and in our own Wordsworth's phrase, "something ever more about to be," the sacred is placed ahead of us. King Arthur will return when England has need of him.

So it is either behind or ahead – apparently far away whenever you seek it. Like performance, spiritual reality exists only as long as you keep participating. You can't *have* the waltz; it's only yours while you're dancing. You can't *hold* a song unless you keep singing. You can't *stay* at the crest of a joke, the moment when the smile breaks into laughter. The shock of being, too, is a performance, something we create with the universe at a moment that has nothing to do with time.

Strange, isn't it, how the bad stuff lingers and the good disappears? I see people every day whose lives have been all but permanently wrecked by trauma, abuse, poverty. Why is it set up this way, so the good won't keep and the bad preserves its noxiousness?

Happily, some goods abide. The most democratic and invisible is language, especially our mother tongue, which we master early and which then keeps arriving for a lifetime. Could we learn to linger in the spiritual goods - the experience of being or insight or love itself – as abidingly as we hang onto "and" and "but"?

The closest answer may be "practice, practice, practice" - the route to Carnegie Hall as well as to the Grail. In the case of the violin, it is clear enough what to practice and how. In the case of being, there are innumerable practices, none of which are guaranteed to yield or extend the experience.

I like to link amazement at existence to every frustration, even the tiny ones. I missed the bus, and come to think of it, how odd that there are buses, people rushing toward them, and a universe in which this is occurring. How strange a thing is frustration itself, this invisible misery.

Such linking will not take you away from practical engagement. It won't make you late for the next bus. It might even make you agitate for more frequent bus service, since you are arranging mentally to step outside the moment of frustration and into its larger context.

And I link the direct experience of being to the boundary between sleep and waking. Every morning when I first swing my feet over onto the floor and stand up, I pause and look around and say to myself, in words or no words, "There is a world here, when there could so easily be nothing. Thank you." Most often, though, the experience comes on its own accord, in and around times of being fully concentrated, on anything.

What is a glimpse of reality like? asks a Zen student. And the answer comes: *Like the bottom falling out of a bucket of water.*

V *is for Vital*

Artists we knew in New York raised their daughters in their loft in Tribeca. This was before the internet had infiltrated the realms of early childhood. One day, our friends took the older girl, Francesca, to enjoy her very first day of summer camp. When they picked her up later, she came running to their arms.

> *Mom! Dad!*, she cried, *you'll never guess what they have at summer camp!*
> *What is it, Sweetie?*, they wondered, thinking, Archery? Pony rides? Swimming in a river?
> *Winning and losing!*, Francesca announced with glee.

There is a certain vitality that can only emerge from boundaries, from rough edges, from contrast. Competition introduced her to an edge she just loved: the thrill of victory, the agony of defeat.

Raised a prince in perfect luxury, the boy who became the Buddha was kept as a kind of prisoner on the palace grounds where he didn't see a wilted flower until the age of 21. One morning he escaped, curious, and was astonished as he wandered the streets of town to see an old, bent person shuffling along. He saw a child ravaged by disease, crouched and begging. He saw people carrying a corpse through the street on a pallet (still a common sight in rural India today). Old age, sickness and death - the stain of human frailty – gave him a world-changing shock and set him on his quest. Unlike

Francesca, the Buddha wasn't overjoyed. But it gave him vital questions and he *had* to find a way to make sense of it. From this awakening came his eventual Awakening and the whole story of his teaching of compassion and joy.

I often ask my patients, "When do you feel most alive?" It's not a question we're trained to keep front and center. Instead there are plans, and regrets, and obligations, and expectations and fears. Someone was in my office recently though, and beat me to it. The first day I met him he launched into a tale of climbing mountains, the gritty ascent, the view of expanse, the thin precious air. Talking about it, his face went from closed, to half awake, to open, to lit.

We knew a couple who were Socialists, committed to a utilitarian, collective life. Yet the wife, an architect, was interested in fine furniture and produced some herself. Given the expensive materials and the hours and hours spent in her shop, we asked her how she justified an interest in these luxury items. "Ah well," she answered, "You have to do what puts the spring in your step."

V is for Victory. Here's a take on victory you may not have thought about, the one Rilke mentions in this poem:

> To be silent. Those who are more inwardly silent
> touch on the roots of speech.
> Someday every syllable they utter
> will be victory
> over what, in the silence, isn't silent,
> over the mocking evil.
> For us to dissolve tracelessly,
> that's why the Word was shown to us.

(I've inserted plurals here – those, they, us – and avoided the he, him of the original, because Rilke was clearly talking about all of us).

Our minds are jumpy with what he calls evil, that is, the deadening stuff of separatist selfhood. In meditation, we notice and allow strange inner imagery, boring repetitions, and all manner of distractions, until they quiet down, and there really is silence.

Silence in turn is a portal, not the last thing at all, but "Jacks-or-better-to-open." It is the exquisite pre-requisite for what the Buddhists call "right speech." Rilke knew it as the victory of being ever more deeply vanquished by the way things are.

W is for Weil

Simone Weil (she pronounced her last name Vay), was a French philosopher and mystic who died in 1943. In my late teens, I read, in a letter of hers to her friend Joé Bousquet:

Il est donné à très peu d'esprits de découvrir que les choses et les êtres existent. Depuis mon enfance je ne désire pas autre chose que d'en avoir reçu avant de mourir la révélation complète. Il me semble que vous êtes engagé dans cette découverte.

*It is given to very few spirits to discover
that things and beings exist.
Since my childhood, I have desired
nothing other than to have received
the complete revelation of this
before dying. It seems to me that you are
engaged in this discovery.*

When I read that, I thought, "She knows about this thing. This experience." I was happy to have the confirmation. But I'm writing this book because I don't think she's quite right. It's not necessarily "given to very few spirits." It's given to everyone, though perhaps in very few moments. Let's have those moments increase in depth and breadth toward the "complete revelation."

My friend Gardiner and I cut gym class one day in 9th grade. We had fled to the opposite end of the school campus where there was a grassy playground, and we were sitting on the swings, happily bored together. Arguing, probably, about some detail of life that is now easily solved by Google but that we enjoyed bickering over in those days. We were taking blades of grass between our thumbs and blowing on them to make a kind of whistle or wailing note. We were just hanging around. There on the playground was a much younger kid, maybe a 5th grader, bouncing a ball alone. Gardiner addressed him:

Hey.
The boy looked up.
This is happening.
The boy looked confused.
You may not realize it, but all this is happening. And years from now maybe you'll remember that this was a real moment, when these two older boys talked to you here on this spot.

The boy shrugged as I recall, not wanting further engagement, and returned to bouncing his ball against the side of the building. We walked away, wondering if he would really remember the episode thirty or forty years on. I still wonder that sometimes, so it marked one of us at least.

"When *are* we?" asks Rilke. He gives us the same challenge Gardiner gave to the kid. In what kind of rare moments can you notice the entirety of things?

Weil had a brilliant academic career ahead of her if she wanted it, but she was too alert to the sufferings of others to lose herself in abstractions. She taught in a poor region; she tried her hand at factory work; she had a stint among migrant workers; she couldn't bear to eat heartily in freedom in London when the French back home under Nazi occupation were made to starve, so kept herself to the rations of those behind enemy lines. Her alertness to the other person was one form of her sense of the real altogether. It is not only the world that is felt to be real, or oneself, but above all, other people. In their reality, they are a call to compassion. "Let us treat the men and women well, treat them as if they were real," says Emerson, "Perhaps they are." Weil felt their reality intensely, and was moved to action. To be fair, Emerson also acted according to his beliefs, and his greatest speeches may be ones we can never read: his extemporaneous abolition talks given to thousands as he criss-crossed the country with vocal and effective outrage.

Weil also wrote about the mystery of the Grail, and for her the Grail is the receptive cup of attention. Instead of only pushing one's own agenda, it is possible to attend to someone else. It is possible to wonder about the other person, to imagine their suffering or delight, and to be involved with them. Attention, for Weil, comes into its highest form in prayer, by which she meant not so much talking and asking for stuff as listening into the circumambient love. She went so far as to say we learn things in school not to use them, but just to develop the capacity for attention, and ultimately for a Grail-style consciousness which alone can receive and comprehend the reality of the world.

In a dream (not a lucid one, but still), I was at my house on a workday morning, just about to go out the front door. As I reached for the handle, the door opened inward on its own. In stepped a tall stick-figure creature, with a huge rectangular box of a head like an old TV set, but blank. The face was just a white, glassy flatness. I thought there radiated a palpable evil from this figure. Somehow though, in spite of my shock and sense of being invaded, I remembered Weil's principle that we can meet all phenomena with a willingness to honor them, with a Grail-like receptiveness. I tried to manifest this attitude toward the intruder, despite the sense of evil. I said to it inwardly: "I am willing to receive any good in you, or to understand your pain." In an instant, the stick-like arms and legs retracted into the head-part, and the whole of it flew around to attach to my back. The box sprouted wings, and I found myself flying out the door and up into a cheering sky.

X *is for Xylophone*

In the alphabets I knew growing up, X was always for
Xylophone or Xerxes. There is probably more human interest
in Xerxes, the Persian emperor against whose outnumbering
hordes the Greeks formed their union and fought the incredible
battle of Thermopylae. Still, it is hard now to visualize those
tales, set so long ago in such a different time.

The benefit of history is not only or not mostly to "learn from
it" – as in learn either not to do the bad things that were done
then, or else to go ahead and do the good things. The highest
value in immersing yourself in the past may be simply to
experience the contrast between that time and this time, which
can make this present day, in which you are reading this
alphabet, stand out against that backdrop in stark relief.

Xerxes was the fellow who got so angry at the water of the
Hellespont, because its tides weren't obedient to his wishes,
that he had the water whipped some 300 lashes. He is also said
to have dropped irons into the water as if to chain it like a
prisoner. The heroism of the Spartans who resisted him made
his victory into defeat and their defeat into victory. If there is a
moral lesson here, I would say it's about the uselessness of
trying to direct or punish the torrent of anyone's psyche. As
soon as I stop trying to control them, every person starts to look
like a miracle.

Lessons and contrasts aside, I'll take Xylophone over Xerxes for my X. Xylophones form part of the magical childhood world, that individualized dawn of civilization we're lucky if we can stretch awake in slowly, an anachronistic jumble of dinosaurs, primitive clay pottery, and spaceships traveling beyond the speed of light. There was a xylophone in the music room at my grade school, and I wouldn't have guessed there was more than one in the world. It was called "The Xylophone," a unique human achievement like "The Empire State Building." I also wouldn't have known that by its Greek sources (ah, those heroes, again, freed into the flow of watery language, un-slowed by a Persian tyrant's chains) it means, the "voice of the wood."

"Who makes the solid tree trunks sound again," is how Frost characterizes the ovenbird. Wood does have a voice. Trees growing close enough together will sigh and groan when the wind makes them fret against one another. Then there are the wooden instruments, from oboes to violins. When Pinocchio learned to speak the truth, he became no longer a wooden puppet but a real boy.

The Xylophone world, as we could call our total project, is not a dead-wood world of sullen and inarticulate things, but a world of voices and meanings. Like the voices (not in sound) that speak to the Kogi from every rock and field and skyscape. We can learn to hear these voices again, and to share our own.

And X is for the X that marks a spot. Like the place on the map where the treasure is buried. Each of us inscribes an X, marking our presence on earth, simply by being alive. Your human life marks the world. To get a preliminary feeling for this, you can notice your body in space: in this chair, not that one, and then be open to impressions from the place around you. Be willing for an exchange of blessings to occur, just by your presence. Locate yourself in time: at your exact age, somewhere between birth and death, sensing into this moment in the earth's history. Be willing to experience an exchange of blessings between yourself and this time — this day, this season, this era.

Grounding ourselves in a particular crossroads of time and space helps us to fully give ourselves to the earth. We may "come from afar," in Wordsworth's phrase, but we are here now and this place, for all its troubles, is good. That is the buried treasure.

is for

yes

Yea, yeah, yay, yup – they are variants of the same affirmative. They all seem like shortened versions of yes.

They are not.

In terms of the history of the words, it is just the reverse. Yes came later, and is a lengthened version of those "s"-less forms.

The "s" of "yes" is from somewhere else altogether. It long ago got tacked onto the end of the yea words to make "yeas", which got boiled down to "yes."

So what does the "s" mean? Its source was an ancient Indo-European root that means (wait for it:) *Being*. Oh yeah, *Being*. *To be*. In fact, the "s" of "yes" is the same "s" as the "s" of "is."

Every time we say Yes, we are saying some form of, "Yay for existence!" or, "Yeah, it is what it is," or, "Yea, let it be so," or "Yup, here we go."

Yes, to the comfy plunking of the clothes in the dryer. Yes, to the red dawn. Yes, to the *chip-burr* of the thrush up at dawn and also reliably repetitive.

And yes to the loss of all I love. It is no help to dwell in the heartbroken no. What are we going to deny? Torture? War? Poverty? Discrimination of all kinds? Climate change and all its devastation? Our weirdest thoughts and fantasies? Our talents? The enormous love available and giveable? Might as well acknowledge and affirm what is. It is so. I may not like it; I may not understand it; I may have to change it; I may have to accept it. It is so. Yes.

Ram Dass used to say, "The world is perfect and complete just as it is right now – which includes your passion and actions to improve it." Yaas!

The strangest Yes for me was that time in Calcutta, when I was living briefly with the Missionaries of Charity. It was the middle of the night, and I was nearly delirious with dehydration from dysentery and fever. I was running back and forth from my thin pallet in a rooftop shed to the rooftop toilet, then returning a dozen times to flop down in a mess of tangled sheets I couldn't help soiling. At one point I couldn't make it back from the toilet to the shed, and lay down on the bare cement roof, clutching my stomach. As I looked up, the stars were directly above me, a clear cold night, the wind opening up the sky above the pervasive scent and smog of Calcutta's street fires. The stars were there, and it seemed they were very close, or even that I was up, up, and floating among them. I wondered if it was possible to accept being alive, including the suffering and poverty and dying all around me. I wanted and continue to want suffering to be over soon – however long it takes in practice. But there was a Yes up there anyway, right in the midst of everything, a peace beyond understanding.

Y is for You. You has a special function. This word, or rather its basic gesture of direct address, calls the person to whom it is spoken into existence. The parents say to the baby, "Look at YOU!" and the baby arrives.

That early armed services recruitment sign was brilliant. It showed the old man pointing at the viewer with the caption, "Uncle Sam wants YOU!" When you felt he was pointing at you, you were implicated, and more likely to signup. Uncle Sam, like the doting parents, used the "you" as a call, a finding and evoking, a challenge whether loving or stern. Out of a background of sleepy non-being, out of the fog, you are brought forth by the word as if by a magic spell. The teacher calls your name and you stop staring out the window and arrive where you are.

The Zen dialogues my Dad read to me when I was growing up, like his tales of rabbis and their students, were above all conversations.

Here's a typical Zen dialogue from around 800 AD as told in "The Blue Cliff Record":

> *A monk asked Pa Ling, "What is the Blown Hair Sword?"*
> *Pa Ling said, "Each branch of coral supports the moon."*

These phrases and the connection between them are not meant to be understood with our normal concepts and mental structures, but during such demanding interchanges a spark arose between teacher and student – a profound sense of each other. That was the teaching.

In our New York days I worked for a while as a proofreader in a huge law firm. It was the midnight shift, the graveyard shift, the lobster shift. A particularly messy, complex draft of an agreement, covered in lines showing where text should go with ambiguous crossouts and substitutions, had resisted my bleary-eyed efforts. I just couldn't see what went where. Another proofreader, a friend, was working at a desk across the room from where I sat, and I asked if she could help. She rose slowly (the lobster shift, so called because we got sluggish and moved like lobsters in the wee hours) and slowly shuffled toward me. As she approached, the page before me swam up from confusion to clarity, and I saw just how it was to be organized, and what referred to what, and what went where. By the time she'd arrived by my side, the text had all fallen into place.

Thanks! I said, *It's all come clear.*
Glad I could help, she replied and turned back to her seat.

The way we come into focus when addressed also means that when un-addressed we cease to be. Patients often tell me that they were ignored or even, so to speak, de-existed by their families of origin and actively made not to be. Kristin, a patient I saw for years, remembered how her violent, insanely abusive grandfather never addressed her by her given name. He would call her by other names invented just to mock and belittle her. He also did something I've heard from many adult survivors: he would address her in the third person, saying for instance, "She's going to turn over now." This had the effect of both making her feel under compulsion and making her feel she didn't, couldn't speak, since there was no first-to-second person stance between her grandfather and her. In less horrific situations, too, we can easily feel disappeared in a group, a work meeting for instance, as soon as our comments go unheard or unanswered. We effectively cease to be.

Martin Buber wrote about the I-Thou relationship and the benefits of addressing others, including the non-human worlds, and letting yourself be addressed. Dialogue brings you forth, and you bring the others forth, just as sunlight provokes the seed to open and the stalk to rise and the leaf to unfurl and the flower and fruit to come. Goethe in a fairy tale has a character ask, "What is more enlivening than light?" and the answer comes, "Conversation."

Here's the start of Psalm 19 in the King James Version:

> *The heavens* declare *the glory of God; and the firmament* sheweth *his handywork.*
> *Day unto day* uttereth *speech, and night unto night* sheweth *knowledge.*

I've emphasized the four verbs on which this passage hangs. All of them, in the original Hebrew, refer to some kind of speech (shew as in "show evidence, affirm"). So even the non-human world, the skies and the times, are in dialogue or conversation. They address one another and so grow more present, their interchange becoming wordless praise of the "LORD," meaning the you and I of being itself.

And Y is for *you*, dear Reader! I have enjoyed writing these reflections on how to intensify being and grow more in love with the world. But I also want them to be read. I'm writing to you.

Z *is for Zigzag*

Being, as we've often noticed, is not a thing or a fact. It is rather the precondition for all things and facts, and their fulfillment, too. Still, our minds and our language are structured to handle objects and facts. So being seems to require zigzags to approach it and trick it into appearance.

We also need zigzags the way we need special glasses to look at the sun during an eclipse, because we can't endure the sledgehammer of reality straight on:

> *Tell all the truth but tell it slant —*
> *Success in Circuit lies:*
> *Too bright for our infirm Delight*
> *The Truth's superb surprise.*

This is how Emily Dickinson put it. The lines suggest that she herself had already advanced to the point where she could perceive or guess at all the truth, and also had the mastery to titrate its delivery to others.

She's the same one who said:
> *I find ecstasy in living – the mere sense of living*
> *is joy enough.*

I don't think the zigzag is forever. Right now, we need alternation, hiding, peekaboo and delay as we adjust our inner eye to the sunrise. We're constituted currently so as to need to find it and lose it and find it again. As we strengthen the vector of attention beyond its habitual steady collapse, as improvisation becomes the un-norm, we will iron out the zigzags into a singing road.

So much depends
upon a red wheelbarrow.
William Carlos Williams

Our final letter is A; we couldn't leave it out! But it won't stand for Astonishment even if this book is the Alphabet of Astonishment. Let's have it stand for *a*, as in a mote of dust, a pickle, a copse, a corpse, a galaxy, a world. It is "a" as the indefinite article, so called, though the whole point of "a" is a definitive selection and what used to be known as the scandal of particularity.

One big difference between *the* and *a* is that specificity-with-in-multiplicity in *a*. "The pear" might be the only pear, like The

Xylophone, or the pear that blows away all others, or the pear already in question, as in: "Since he'd gone to so much trouble bringing it to me on camel-back from across the desert, I accepted the pear." It's over-emphasized, over-known. *A* pear, on the other hand, is one of many pears, the more interesting for its being one plucked from out of a series.

Kristin, the patient whose grandfather wouldn't call her by her real name, wouldn't tell me about a dream. Oh, she referred to her dreams all the time. "I've been having a lot of dreams about mice," she might say, or "My dreams these days are increasingly crystal clear, and increasingly frightening. In some of them I have different bodies, not human or even animal, but more like glue or mud." She seemed unable to descend from these generalities to describe *a* dream, a specific dream, any one dream, and this avoidance seemed part of her overall difficulty which she herself labeled as, "having a hard time incarnating, you know?"

I don't put much stock in standard dream interpretation, but I found myself eager to hear her take hold and take form, and come to earth in this particular way, by describing a dream. A single dream. One dream. We talked about it, this hankering of hers for the general case, and my hankering for a particular. She saw her problem with particularity as a legacy of her traumatic past and her habit of dissociation.

So she tried. She'd say, "OK, Mr. Doctor Psychologist, I had a dream last night. *A* dream. OK? This one was a doozey. Probably it came because of my fight with that no-good co-worker of mine yesterday. We go way back, you know. In fact, you don't know this, but I first met him years before we worked together at an outdoor, neighborhood party, the annual block party. They had to get town permits to close off the street. Back then I was still with Harry. You remember, Harry was the one with the antique store that went bust." On and on it would go, a dream deferred, regardless of my interjections, until the session ended.

Generality served her derealization and depersonalization. A sense of the real began to grow only when she came increasingly into relationship with *a* moment, *a* dream, *an* event at work, *a* window box of violets, *a* dog from the pound, *a* lost childhood, *a* lost love.

> —*But there's a tree, of many, one,*
> *A single field which I have look'd upon ....*
>   Wordsworth, "Ode: Intimations"

This was the passage that threw William Blake into "almost hysterical rapture" according to Crabbe Robinson, a friend of Blake's who read Wordsworth's poem aloud to him.

In selecting a lovely pine to admire and admiring it for decades as I slowly biked past it on hundreds of mornings on my way into Great Barrington, I put myself at risk with that one tree by loving it heedlessly. I did not think that it might not always be there on my right, rising up soon after the road flattened out below Butternut Hill as I rode past. Without any all-things-must-pass kind of thoughts toward this tree which gave me such joy with its two vast trunks so obviously flung heavenward in August's welcome-the-day-with-a-shout sort of way, and in loving this lithe twin tower of a tree, a heroic White Pine, I was at risk and unawares. When they cut it, freshly dead and quickly dismembered, chipped to smithereens and hauled off before 8am, I didn't stop my bike to ask the workmen why, partly because of the tears and partly because I saw the black core of some dismembered pieces, and now that tree is not there.

Every year, in the Loebner Prize competition, computer programming enthusiasts design programs to fool judges who don't know if they are in dialogue with a computer or with a human being. The judges type in their questions, and they get answered either by a human typing back to them, or by a computer whose program coughs up "answers." The judges have to discern whether they are in conversation with a computer program or with a human being.

The big Loebner Prize goes to the programming team whose program fools the most judges into thinking they are conversing with a human. It's all based on Alan Turing's 1949 challenge: if you can't tell whether you're writing back and forth with a person or a computer, then there is, functionally, no difference, and we can say that the computer is intelligent.

Brian Christian, in his charming book, *The Most Human Human*, tells of his effort to win, not the well-known Loebner Prize for the most human-seeming computer, but another much less well known prize. He aimed at the prize for "Most Human Human," which goes to the human who convinces the most judges that, yes, they are in conversation with a living, breathing, feeling-ful, intelligence-endowed human being.

The computer programs in use these days no longer come up with their own algorithmically constructed sentences based on matching grammatical forms from their database to words or phrases in the judges' questions. Rather, they search the Internet on the spot for real-life, human-composed answers to questions similar to those the judges are asking. So the "computer's" remarks are all actual human remarks, sourced from all over the globe. How could Christian prove he was a human against that kind of competition? How could he get the judges to distinguish between his personal, human replies and the computer's replies cunningly spliced together from other real human sentences the computer sourced in that instant online?

Christian focused on the fact that computers do not have, and therefore cannot convey to the judges, the sense of being one fleshly human person. The responses they serve up come from many humans, but they are not the responses of *a* human. In philosopher Bernard Reginster's words, the computers do not have the trick of "being one self, any self." Christian won the prize for Most Human Human by conveying in his typed responses the coherency of one person, with a biography, sitting there at a screen, in a Loebner competition conference room, on a particular day with its particular weather, typing his heart out.

A man had nearly drowned. They hauled him up, and his body was pale, limp, apparently gone. It was touch and go as they tried to revive him. Everyone bent over him, eager to bring him back, anxious to detect the slightest pulse or movement, any sign of returning life. This story is told in Dickens's *Our Mutual Friend*, but it's Giles Deleuze, once again, who brought it to my attention in one of his last writings. The Dickens character, Riderhood, is thoroughly unlovable. Yet in his near-dead state everyone forgets his nastiness and urgently strives to bring him back. They feel the tender sanctity of this one human life, with its untold potential, and they love him. As their efforts are successful, and he begins to resume strength and consciousness, they immediately loathe him again.

What Deleuze points out in his essay is that those hovering over the near-dead man do wish to bring back *a* life, Riderhood's specific life, even if they didn't like what he'd made of life so far.

Now we know that Deleuze himself was about to die as he wrote about the Riderhood episode and issues of ultimate value were on his mind as never before. Deleuze goes on in his essay, letting his writing hover over the qualities of small children and how each of them has *a* life, even before they have quite individuated into definite characters and personalities.

So the Dickens character is near death but coming back to life; Deleuze, focusing on the story, is near death and not fixing to return; the children he describes have just entered life eager for more. What Deleuze seems to be after is a pure incarnation-potential within each of us: something specific but unsullied and present in us whether we're old and battered or newly minted. He's going into the scandal of particularity even more intimately than Brian Christian, that very human human. Deleuze is pointing us to an *a* that we may only rarely find, though we often love one house, one person, one job. He's close to the Zen masters when they dare their students for instance to, "Show me your original face before your grand-parents were born."

My dream-avoider in therapy, Kristin, desperately wanted to find an unbroken continuity between a freshness she knew must have been there before her abuse began and a freshness that must still be her nature now.

It was hard to locate, as she was hard to locate for herself. She said the wires of her inner circuitry were not just crossed: the circuit-board had melted. She didn't know one day from the next, and chronically got lost, terrified that if she were in a spot on earth and at a certain time, she would be found by her abuser (now long dead). She had constructed weird worlds and realms in which she wandered, day and night, unfindable. What was her original face, she was asking, before her grandfather tortured and disfigured her?

She was a successful lawyer in her 50's, but had been unable to bring her many social/professional skills to bear in her personal life. She had always lived alone.
Kristin recalled playing dollhouse games with a distant cousin on just two occasions in childhood. These visits had assumed enormous significance during the hundreds of occasions when

her grandfather was beating and sexually abusing her. She would "go to the cousin's" in her mind, escaping the scene of abuse.

Now, in therapy, through her deliberate acts of memory and extension, the remembered love for this cousin and their imaginary doll-world began to assume a different significance, not involving escape. It turned slowly into a feeling for the coherence of a whole grown-up world.

She started joining groups, then having outings with new-made friends, then – so hesitantly – online dating. Finally, one day she surprised me by walking into her session arm in arm with a man she had met online. Last I heard, they were still together.

From the first day, Kristin had what it took to overcome her troubles. One special feature: she would insist that I be a person toward her, not just a clinician, so that she could become a person herself, and not just a patient. Normally gruff, she was also hair-trigger sensitive, and would respond warmly to any uptick in my relatedness to her. "Now you are Michael," she might say with a note of triumph in her voice, "and you are talking to me, Kristin." After a lifetime of hovering, the clarity of her aim helped her, in her words again, "to land on a planet."

The minister-farmer-inventor Jonathan Fisher, of Blue Hill, Maine, painted these words on the face of a clock he built by hand in 1792:

Beholder, thou art NOW alive!

He was thrifty and hard-working and collaborative in a world that seemed to offer endless natural gifts. We are alive in a time where the earth's spiritual and physical atmosphere is threatened to a degree Fisher would be unlikely to imagine. What can we create now, together with each other and with all earth's kingdoms? First, we must realize the living miracle in our being here to collaborate.

Reader, it is so unlikely that you and I would create a sentence together, but here we are.

~

Quotations instead of a conclusion

I shall climb through the clouds and exist.
John Keats

Why are there things, rather than nothing?
Martin Heidegger

In the corridor of the school where I teach, I sometimes find myself whispering, "I exist. Exist!" And everything would go quiet.
Psychology grad student

Each mortal thing does one thing and the same,
Deals out that being indoors each one dwells.
Gerard M. Hopkins

I was dissolving into what I saw, and at the same time I was feeling my individuality intensely, as if for the first time. I was coming into being.
Ian McEwan

It is strange to be here. The mystery never leaves you alone.
John O'Donohue

To be here is much.
Rainer M. Rilke

The deer. That they are there.
George Oppen

Our noisy years seem moments in the being
Of the eternal Silence.
William Wordsworth

Moments of Being.
Virginia Woolf

Yet there is a depth in those brief moments which constrains
us to ascribe more reality to them than to all others.
Ralph W. Emerson

You are dreaming. I am awake.
Sri Nisargadatta

This is what our society needs — not new ideas and
inventions, important as these are; and not geniuses and
supermen, but persons who can "be", that is, persons who
have a center of strength within themselves.
Rollo May

Even the flowers don't come back, or the green leaves.
There are new flowers, new green leaves.
There are other beautiful days.
Nothing comes back, nothing repeats itself, because
everything is real.
Alberto Caeiro

*Joy is nothing other than the feeling of reality… Sadness
is nothing other than the weakening or disappearance of
this feeling.*
Simone Weil

*[H]uman kind
Cannot bear very much reality.*
T. S. Eliot

*Truth [in communicating with a terminally ill patient] is
much more in a relationship than in words…to be able to
just share, perhaps not say anything. Because, quite often,
all that somebody [on their deathbed] wants is for you to
just stay there, appreciate that what they're facing is very
hard. And we don't want to smooth everything over and
say everyone is cheerful in a hospice, but we do want to say
things are real and reality, when you come to terms with it,
has an extraordinary amount of joy hidden there.*
Dame Cicely Saunders
founder of Hospice

*Living, there is no happiness in that. Living: carrying
one's painful self through the world.
But being, being is happiness. Being: Becoming a
fountain, a fountain on which the universe falls like warm
rain.*
Milan Kundera

The typhoon has joy in being what it is.
Giles Deleuze

*I want to live forever at the very moment the unfolding
idea comes pouring through me and out into expression.*
Wayne Koestenbaum

Who pours himself forth like a fountain,
The Knowing knows him.
Rainer M. Rilke

To deal with things knowledge of things is needed. To deal
with people, you need insight, sympathy.
To deal with yourself, you need nothing.
Be what you are – conscious being – and don't stray away
from yourself.
Sri Nisargadatta

Say to the flowing water, I AM.
Rainer M. Rilke

Before Abraham was, I AM.
Jesus of Nazareth

And God said unto Moses, I AM THAT I AM: and he
said, Thus shalt thou say unto the children of Israel, I AM
hath sent me unto you.
Exodus 3:14

In the name of the bee,
the butterfly
and the breeze,
Amen.
Emily Dickinson

This is when we entered what I came to think of as Plan
"Be," existing only in the present.
Amy K. Rosenthal,
terminal cancer patient

It's enough for me to be sure that you and I exist at this moment.
Gabriel Garcia Marquez

The first question which we have a right to ask will be, 'Why is there something rather than nothing?'
Gottfried Leibniz

How extraordinary that anything should exist.
Ludwig Wittgenstein

But I felt: you are an I,
you are an Elizabeth,
you are one of them.
Why *should you be one, too?...*
I knew that nothing stranger
had ever happened, that nothing
stranger could ever happen....
How - I didn't know any
word for it - how "unlikely"....
Elizabeth Bishop

I will never forget the appearance within me, which I have never yet told anyone, when I was present at the birth of my self-awareness. I can give the exact time and place. It was morning, and I stood as a very young child in the doorway, looking left toward the woodpile. Suddenly the inner view, 'I am an I' shot before me like a bolt of lightning from heaven, and has remained ever since, luminously.
Jean Paul

The universe consists in a communion of subjects, not a
collection of objects.
Thomas Berry

An empty day without events.
And that is why
it grew immense
as space. And suddenly
happiness of being
entered me.
Ana Swir

Thy life is a miracle.
William Shakespeare

Just to be is a blessing. Just to live is holy.
Abraham Joshua Heschel

I find ecstasy in living – the mere sense of living is
joy enough.
Emily Dickinson

All in a few days, it was a nameless storm, a hurricane in
the spirit (like that time at Duino), all that was fiber and
fabric in me cracked. Eating was not to be thought of, God
knows who fed me. But now it is. Is. Is.
Amen.
Rainer M. Rilke,
in a letter to Princess Marie von Thurn u. Taxis,
Feb 11, 1922, on finishing the Duino Elegies

Summation or reverberation depends on there being a certain quantity of reflecting back to the individual on the part of the trusted therapist (or friend) who has taken the (indirect) communication. In these highly specialized conditions the individual can come together and exist as a unit, not as a defence against anxiety but as an expression of I AM, I am alive, I am myself. From this position, everything is creative.
D. W. Winnicott

When are we? And when does He turn the earth and the stars toward our being?
Rainer M. Rilke

To be or not to be?
William Shakespeare

I LIKE TO BE
name of a painting by Rose Wylie, 2020

It is given to very few spirits to discover that things and beings exist. Since childhood, I have desired nothing other than to have received the full revelation of this before dying. It seems to me that you, too, are engaged in this discovery.
Simone Weil

~

Acknowledgements

Many thanks (uncountably many) to all friends, students, teachers, colleagues and others who gave me encouragement in this writing and who alerted me to the miracle of being here.

To Rody who challenged me from time to time with, "Dad, you haven't finished that book yet?" – and whose own existence is a marvel. To Asher, also a marvel.

To those who expressed doubt, making me ask again, "Do I have to do this?" and to answer, "Yes."

To Joseph Rubano, Paul Weiss, Courtney Maum, Andrea Panaritis, Claire Hicks and all who gave preliminary versions their sympathetic attention. A special thanks to Lora Vatalaro, whose suggestions and encouragement made the book markedly better.

To David Spangler, Georg Kühlewind, Chris Bamford, Fred Paddock: friends in all weathers.

To members of the Tuesday Meditation Group, who inspired this work again and again.

To Jeremy Berg, Susan Sherman and the Lorian Press: a welcome home. And to Gabriele Franziska Götz, who made it beautiful.

To whatever being, in a dream, handed me a paperback and said, "It should be a light book, called BE."

To the earth itself: no earth, no book.

Above all to Holly Morse, my lifelong instructor in the art of love. She makes the universe possible.

Imprint

BE: An Alphabet of Astonishment
by Michael Lipson

design
Gabriele Franziska Götz, ambulantdesign.nl

font
DTL Fleischmann DOT

publisher
Lorian Press LLC

~

ISBN 978-1-939790-57-6